to Jane

CW00865244

HOW GOD LOOKS

IF YOU DON'T START IN CHURCH

A technologist's view

❖ ❖

MICHAEL RANKEN

Michael Ranken

CAIRNS PUBLICATIONS

SHEFFIELD

2001

ISBN 1 870652 32 0

Cairns Publications
Dwylan, Stryd Fawr, Harlech,
Gwynedd, LL46 2YA
www.cottercairns.co.uk
office@cottercairns.co.uk

Typeset in Monotype Baskerville by
Cairns Publications and Strathmore Publishing Services

Printed by Biddles of Guildford

CONTENTS

FOREWORD

Michael Ranken has shown a good deal of patience while this book has been tossed to and fro by the winds of the publishing world, with its delays almost as frustrating as the due processes of the law. But he still wants me to write this Foreword! I do so with pleasure.

Twenty or so years ago I first came across Michael's name when he was looking in detail at the small part of the secular world he knew about, and asking how that connected with his Christian faith. He wanted us to ask ourselves questions which are so easily bypassed in the daily rush. For example, what is there in this food processing laboratory, this school, this engineering works, this sewage farm, that those working there can be thankful for? What goes wrong, and how is it put right? What is the meaning and purpose of this enterprise within the wider community and world? Gratitude, penitence, forgiveness, reconciliation, purpose – all are given attention in every celebration of the central act of Christian worship, the Holy Communion, and are significant in any exploration of Christian faith.

At that time I was helping to train students who would continue with their working lives whilst also entering the ordained ministry of the Church of England. Michael was an ally as I pressed the question, How do your biblical and theological studies *connect* with the language and reality of your everyday secular experience? It is a process still too often honoured by the Church more in the breach than in the observance.

I am glad Michael has continued to work and think on the frontier – often a puzzle, as he says in the Preface, to his colleagues and friends in lab and parish. I am reminded of Alan Ecclestone in Sheffield who was a C. of E. vicar and a member of the British Communist Party, neither institution quite knowing what to make of his membership of the other!

v

I hope Michael will enjoy being reminded of this quotation from the magazine *Theology*, for which he wrote an article on these things in March 1982, and I hope it will whet the reader's appetite for what follows.

"...consider the sewage worker, the dustman, the morgue attendant, the lavatory paper manufacturer, and their share in keeping us healthy, each continually recognizing, acknowledging, accepting, correcting faults – and forgiving them, for in the world 'out there' not so many of the myriad errors that they face are actually left unresolved, provoking guilt...note how much of good 'secular' management techniques attend to the business of bringing errors to light, gently, so that they can be resolved and new life begin. And the sewage worker and the others are doing God's work for us (or is it our work for God?) with real sacrifice of social regard. They work, by and large, as God does, silently and without thanks. By the rest of us, by and large, they are misunderstood, disparaged or ignored. And the work of giving, of creating life, goes on. They are our servants. Isaiah's descriptions fit. Daily they forgive our negligences and ignorances, mostly they do not store them up or hold them against us. That is much more than we deserve, and in that respect too we should see that it is exactly what we say about God."

JIM COTTER
Cairns Publications
Sheffield, March 2001

PREFACE

I am a food technologist and have spent all my working life in and around the food industry. I retired from full-time work in 1997 but I keep up an interest in the profession and the activities of former colleagues, and still do a little consultancy. I have also been an Anglican priest for the past quarter of my life – in Church of England language a non-stipendiary minister or NSM, and, as long as I was at work, a minister in secular employment or MSE.

So I have lived two roles, as food technologist and as priest. But I am only one person, the same person in both roles. Various people have asked, and some still do, how I manage to reconcile either role with the other. In part, this book is a response to that question. It has been some years in the writing, as the things which I see and the ways I want to tell them have changed and developed as I thought about them. While that has been happening, another, deeper reason for writing has emerged: to show some of the *process* by which the reconciliation has been established.

The struggle has not been, as I hear many people say that it is for them, to reconcile the ways of a puzzling and often hostile world with a relatively confident religious faith. For me it is the other way round. My working world is filled with things which I find true and trustworthy: it is the things said by religion which are obscure and puzzling.

All along I have been guided by one simple conviction: that if religion is right to claim, as Christianity certainly does claim, that the truths which it tells are universally true, that 'God is everywhere', then those truths must be true throughout all of science and technology also. The converse should also be true: that all of the things which are known to be true in science or technology should be true in every other area of existence and fully consistent, visibly and in detail, with all the truths of religion.

vii

That is what I have had to demonstrate to myself and that is what I want to try to demonstrate here.

I have to start from where I am, or was until recently, in the technical world of food production. I shall take ideas and examples from that world, from things in it which I have experienced and things about it which I understand, and I shall mostly do so using the language and the ways of expression which we use in that world all the time. Of course that world and its language are not familiar to everybody. Most other people live their lives in various other parts of this complicated world. Their daily concerns, the things they have to do, and the terms they use while doing them, are all different from mine. But I hope that at least some of what I have to say here about the realities of the part of the world which I inhabit and care about, even if the descriptions sound strange, will nevertheless be recognizable as true also in the experience of other people occupied in very different fields.

MICHAEL RANKEN
Hythe, September 2000

ACKNOWLEDGEMENTS

I cannot begin to list all those whose ideas and comments have helped to form my thinking about these things, but I do want to pay particular thanks to two groups of people for their considerable, if often unknowing, help and encouragement. First, the network which has become the association CHRISM – CHRistians In Secular Ministry – ordained and lay ministers of different denominations, engaged in a wide range of secular jobs, wrestling together with the same questions of how to tell the Christian Good News in and from the working environments which each knows and respects. The other group is the people of Epsom, especially of the parish of St Martin of Tours and St Stephen-on-the-Downs where I was Honorary Curate for eighteen years and where in conversations and sermons many of the thoughts in this book began to be worked out. These all bore much and criticized some; I am grateful to them all for their kindness and patience.

A NOTE ON TREES

How many trees have been used to publish this book? Well, only the pulp is used, which comes from the trimmings: the trunks are used for furniture. A commercially grown soft wood tree produces, on average, about one-sixth of a ton of pulp. Since this book has used about one ton, it has needed six trees to produce it – but of course not all of those six trees. By weight it has needed about three-quarters of one tree. So Cairns Publications is donating the wherewithal for the planting of two trees, in gratitude and recompense.

INTRODUCTION

There are those who say that if what science says is true, then belief in God is not possible; there are others whose religion leads them to deny some of the things which science is now quite sure about. Others again appear to resolve the matter in a kind of schizophrenia. They trust what science says and achieves (or most of it) and at the same time, in some separate part of their minds, they hold religious beliefs which would be in plain conflict with their understanding of science if ever they allowed themselves to make the comparison.

I take none of those positions. What I want to tell, because it is what I see wherever I look, is that there is only one world, one universe. If the things which science believes really are true then they are true everywhere, and if there is a God at all then whatever is true of that God is likewise true everywhere. Neither science nor religion can know all that there is to be known, even if some of their practitioners appear to claim otherwise. They approach things from different directions and see things differently, but what they approach, what is there to be seen, must ultimately be the same for each. There should be no need to split our minds to keep the visions separate. On the contrary, most things are viewed better through two eyes than through one only.

My life and my experience, my thoughts and my vision, cannot be the same as anybody else's, but mine are the only ones that I can properly know about. Much of what I write here, therefore, is in the first person, about what I think and I believe. You will have to make up your own mind, if you want to, about the worth of any of it for yourself.

I write also as a technological person, qualified and competent in some matters, unqualified and incomplete in many others. I shall describe later how this is a proper condition to be in: to be content, at least for the moment, with incomplete and approximate answers to some very significant questions, while continuing to trust one's own competence to deal effectively with other matters of more immediate concern. For I believe that incompleteness and approximation are normal features of the human condition, that none of us can be expert in all the essential activities of our lives. So I write for people all of whom I believe to be as incomplete and approximate as I am, yet each at the same time expert in other fields where I am not.

I lay out my thoughts in three parts. The first part is an attempt to clarify some of the ways my mind works, the relationships between what I think I know and what I believe to be true, and the ways in which such thoughts may be communicated with others. Then in Part 2 I try to set out how all of the things which I believe to be true in my scientific and technological experience are equally true from a religious perspective, congruent with all the essential tenets of my Christian faith. In a final part I try to draw out some general implications.

Part 1:
How I think

❖❖❖❖❖❖❖❖❖❖❖❖❖

1

People and Things

This is where I have to start. I don't believe there is anywhere else that I *can* start.

I am I. I exist. I am here. I think that that is the only thing which I know for certain, perhaps it is the only thing which I *can* know for certain.

Of everything else which I know, or believe, or think I know or believe, it is the same I who does the thinking or the knowing or the believing, and the only one who can.

Of course most of my thoughts, my knowledge, my beliefs do not spring up ready-made inside me; most of them come from someone, from something or somewhere else. But until I accept them and take them in, none of them is mine; as soon as I do accept them they become mine, truly mine, part of me.

I am also the one who has to live my life and the only one who can. Whatever actions, decisions and choices have to be made, I am the one who must make them. I am responsible for every single step of my life. Some of the choices do seem pretty forced, as if I don't have any options, but that is never quite true even in the hardest cases. I always have the option to refuse, to opt out, or to do nothing – and to take the consequences whatever they may be.

The only way I can make those choices is with *my* brain, *my* mind; and all I have to help me make them is *my* own knowledge, thoughts, and beliefs. I also know, by now, that what is in my mind never seems to be quite enough, or reliable enough, to get all the decisions and choices that I have to make quite right. For one thing, I never seem to have enough information, not even enough

5

of the things which are there to be known if only I had taken the trouble, or had had the opportunity, to learn them. For another, it too often seems that something I believe to be true and reliable actually isn't; and I don't always find out about that. Nevertheless, however incomplete is my knowledge, however wrong may be some of my beliefs, and however I unknowingly mislead myself, still I am the only one who has to lead my life and the only one responsible for it. I have to get on with it.

> *I am the one who has to live my life, even though I can never get things quite right.*

The Universe

Of course there is a whole universe outside me, different from me, not-I. There is the physical universe of people, creatures, and organisms, and of objects, places, countries, oceans, planets, and galaxies. There are the forces which operate in that universe, and the thoughts and ideas which other people have about it all.

The universe affects and influences me in a multitude of ways, most of which seem to be quite beyond my control, most of which *are* beyond my control. I do not know what many of the influences are. There must be plenty which I am not aware of. Some parts of the universe are so far away from me – away in physical space or absent from my mind – that they seem to influence me not at all. None the less, I trust the proposition that even the flutter of a butterfly's wing in an English meadow exerts sufficient gravitational force to move Mount Kilimanjaro very slightly. So I suppose that everything in the universe has some effect upon me, however tiny, and I have some effect, however tiny, on everything else.

And I depend, almost absolutely, upon that universe outside me. Whether I run, stand or lie down, it supports me. It provides the food I eat and the air I breathe. Most of my thoughts and my feelings arise from things that I see and hear in it. I cannot possibly live without it.

It does also seem quite possible that there are other universes beyond this one, about which it is entirely beyond my capacity, and perhaps beyond anybody else's, to know anything. They may exist but I cannot know it.

Other People

You, of course, and everybody else, are parts of that universe which is outside me.

You, like everything else, influence and affect me, in some ways which I may know and in others which I don't. You influence me more strongly the closer we are together (in every sense), less strongly the further we are apart.

From your point of view, I am sure, I am part of the universe which is outside you. I, like everything else, influence and affect you, in some ways which you may know and in others which you don't. I influence you more strongly the closer we are together, less strongly the further we are apart.

And I suppose – I think quite reasonably – that everything I just wrote about myself is true likewise of you and of all people. Each and all of us are responsible for our own life. We are free within certain limits which we can never quite define, yet always incomplete and fallible.

Also, we are all different people, standing in different places, with different histories. Your knowledge and abilities are not the same as mine, your beliefs are not all the same, nor your deficiencies, nor the things which you don't know. You have to live your life and make your decisions, based upon what you know and what you believe – and, like me, you can never get everything completely right.

> *I have no means to see inside you, so I cannot* know *that these things are true of you or anybody else, but I do* believe *it.*

2

Knowledge and Belief

If I gain new knowledge or think new thoughts about anything
outside me, I must first receive an impression, a thought, an idea,
from the thing outside me, and then bring the impression into my
mind to think about it. From then on, all further thoughts take
place inside my mind and are *my* thoughts. All I have to think those
thoughts *with* is the same mind, and whatever thoughts, beliefs, and
ideas there may already be inside it. There is no other way.

So what do I think goes on inside me while I am thinking – or
imagining or dreaming?

Information

Much of what I know has come to me through my senses – the
things which I see, hear, touch, smell, and taste.

I should be careful. Most of the time I trust my senses and the
information they give me; but my senses may be defective. Some
of the defects, if I know about them, can be corrected (so I now
wear bifocal spectacles) or allowed for (I now know that my palate
is relatively sensitive to certain flavours and less sensitive to some
others, which I ought to keep in mind when I have to do tasting
tests – or sensory analysis, to use the jargon). But there may be
other defects which I don't know about, in the workings of my
eyes, ears, nose, tongue, or skin, or in the nerves that transfer physical sensations to my brain, or in the systems in my brain that turn
sensory impressions into feelings, and the feelings into words like
hot, green, salty, loud, or smooth. The information which I
believe that I get from my senses is actually the interpretation
which my mind has made of a certain sequence of experiences,
more or less correctly or incorrectly.

Other information comes from things which happen to me or

around me. These things also reach me in the first place through my senses, causing unique and transitory first impressions and feelings. Information about other people's thoughts and ideas, and of happenings where I was not present, comes from books and newspapers, television or what people tell me, passing through my senses of sight and hearing, often so unconsciously or automatically that I don't seem to notice it happening. Afterwards there is only my memory of the impressions and feelings – and that memory too may be unreliable.

Emotions

I read in my encyclopaedia that "no one, including the most capable scientist, fully understands what the source of the emotions is." But I know that I have them, and that I sometimes have little control over them. Feelings such as fear, anger, sadness, pleasure, contentment, love, and hate keep surging within me. Sometimes one or another seems to predominate, sometimes several come mixed together. Often they are unexpected and I cannot always say what it was that caused me to feel like that. Hardly ever can I avoid or prevent them, though often I can and do encourage or enhance them. Sometimes the emotion takes over completely, overriding all conscious thinking, and causing me to behave in ways I did not want and certainly did not choose.

So my feelings must be included amongst the important things which I don't know properly and can't always control, but which significantly affect what I think and do.

Truth

I ought to check each piece of new information against all the other things which I already know or believe to be true, and if it appears to be consistent with them all, if it fits, only then should I say that I know it, and know that it is true.

If the fit appears to be approximate or incomplete, I ought to 'keep it in mind' for further checking. If I find later that it does fit, well and good, I can accept it as true. But I may forget, or fail to check properly, and continue to keep it in mind as if it were true.

Either way, I will *believe* it to be true, and trust it in the same way that I trust the things which I *know*. And, again, I can be wrong.

> *Wasn't it Mark Twain who said, "It ain't the things we don't know that cause the trouble, it's the things we know that ain't so"?*

Conversely, there are some true things which I do know, but have forgotten that I know them. The forgotten thoughts and memories, they say, remain active, deep inside, affecting decisions I make in ways of which I am not consciously aware.

> *I am told that my mind never completely forgets anything, that every-thing I ever knew is stored away somewhere. But I can't always make the mental connections to bring them back from wherever they were put, unless something re-minds me. The psychologists say more: I have buried some things so deep in my unconscious mind that I will never remember them, except perhaps through psychoanalysis or some violent shock.*

Imagination and Ideas

As well as things in the physical world and things within myself which I have learned about directly or indirectly through my senses, there are things which I *imagine* in my mind. Those things may or may not exist in the 'real' world, and I may have no means of checking whether they do or not. So I cannot say that I *know* if they are true. But I certainly can *believe* that they are.

I also think *about* things which I know, or believe, or imagine. I have *ideas* about them, about what they may be like, about possible connections and explanations.

Of course I should check my ideas and my imaginings in the same ways that I should check facts and beliefs, but I don't always. It turns out, again, that some of them when they are checked appear to be true, whilst others which I believe to be true and fail to check, actually are false.

Now, how do I share these thoughts, of all kinds, with other people?

Words

I write here as I mostly think, in the English language. All human thinking and all expressions of thought have to be done in some language or other, and of course English is not the only one. Some of my friends speak and think better in French or Italian or German, some are fluent in the rather different languages of computer programming or pure mathematics. What I want to say applies to all of these and to every other language in use around the world.

Words themselves bring some problems. First, there never are enough of them, in any language, to say everything that we sometimes want to say, or to express some of our more subtle shades of meaning properly. I might occasionally invent a new word to express what I mean, but that will work only if other people can be brought to understand and accept the new word and its special meaning. On the other hand, I don't want to be bothered with too many different words for things which really are quite similar; so it is often convenient to take a word which I know already and give it more than one shade of meaning. I use *similes* and *metaphors*.

As I was taught at school, a *simile* is when we say that so-and-so is *like* such-and-such. So, "The legs of my chair are like spindles" contains a simile which applies quite well to the chair I am sitting on now.

A *metaphor* is when we say that so-and-so *is* such-and-such, so that "such-and-such" becomes what we call it. A metaphor has the curious property of being obviously true for its immediate purpose and at the same time false when you examine it more closely.

"My chair has spindly legs" is a double metaphor. Both metaphors are true – the chair has legs, and the legs are spindly, but they are also not true – 'legs' are the movable things attached to my hips and the things attached to the seat of my chair are not at all the same; 'spindly' ought to mean 'like the thing you use for spinning cotton', which the things on my chair resemble only slightly.

But although it will break down if I take it too far, a good metaphor, especially when I meet it for the first time, can 'open my eyes' (what a good metaphor!) to similarities and connections between things which I had not noticed before.

Stories

So far I have been describing individual pieces of information or ideas, how I discover and test them, how I understand and describe them. But what I have in my mind is not just pieces of information. The pieces are arranged, ordered, and cross-connected into patterns, some of them quite complex. Many, perhaps most, of the patterns are in the form of *stories*.

When I make up or compose a story in my imagination, I 'see' connections among some of the pieces of information, facts, ideas, and remembered events; as I 'see' the connections, I may also 'find' explanations for some of them. What I 'see' and what I 'find' become the *ideas* which join the pieces together into a coherent account.

After I first imagine any story, I tell it to myself, often many times, occasionally altering it here and there to improve it. Then I tell it to others, maybe many more times, maybe changing it more as it goes along. I believe that every story which I have ever heard or read or repeated, indeed every story ever told, was formed and told and developed in this way, and that most of them continue to live and to grow in this way. For almost every story also, there are alternative versions, other ways of telling it, in which the characters may have different names, and some of the circumstances may appear different, but the general shape is the same and the same point is made.

Rather like a metaphor but much more complex, a story can have several *layers of meaning*.

There is the *surface meaning*, contained in the surface details: the words, the form of the story, its contents, and the facts, beliefs, and ideas which connect them together. There is the moral or conclusion or 'point' which the story more or less obviously conveys. A good story also has *inner meanings*, telling more than appears obviously on the surface, as characters and features in the story are discovered to represent other ideas, indirectly and more or less subtly, or where more profound conclusions and morals are seen than the simpler ones on the surface. The inner meanings need not always be recognized by the hearer or even by the teller, but may nevertheless be understood and conveyed unconsciously. Allegories and parables are examples: they are good stories on the surface but usually told much more for their inner meanings.

> *As Bruno Bettelheim tells it in* The Uses of Enchantment, *fairy stories are perhaps the best examples of all. These are the stories which* everybody *knows, which children want to hear over and over again, and which adults love to remember and re-tell all their lives. And in every culture there are similar stories. Why? Because not only are they good stories on the surface, but their inner meanings, the truths about life which lie beneath the surface, are exactly the right ones to be told to and absorbed by children, and re-minded to their elders. Fairy tales tell the great truths of how the hero – the child – however puzzled and frightened at first, can always win in the end, after risky and danger-ous adventures; how goodness and beauty do triumph over wickedness and ugliness; how determination, wit, and ingenuity (especially those of an uncomplicated child, when helped by mysterious powers like those of the fairies or the little forest creatures) can overcome even the most threatening of grown-up giants or stepmothers.*

Now if I ask whether a story is true, things begin to be complic-ated, for the rules about truth in the different levels of a story are not all the same.

I usually start by checking, in the usual ways, whether the sur-face details, the characters, and the data, are factually or scientifically or historically true, corresponding reasonably closely with what I know or believe to be true in other contexts. If they are, I may go on to take it that the conclusion drawn, the point of the story, the surface meaning, follows logically and is therefore also true.

But that is not always appropriate. In many stories the surface details are plainly fanciful, even false, yet the conclusion which they lead to nevertheless does appear to be true. Perhaps many of the funny stories, and the rude ones, which I so enjoy, are like that.

Others again, like the fairy stories, are plainly fanciful on the surface, but have inner meanings which I can recognize and accept deep in my unconscious, with my conscious mind only barely aware of them. However fanciful the surface appearance, however factually untrue, I do take those stories to be true at a deep, hidden level – 'profoundly' true.

From which I conclude that I can *always take a story to be true when its inner meaning is true,* whether I recognize that consciously or not, and whether I accept the surface truth of it or not. Conversely, if the inner meanings of any story do not accord with what I unconsciously believe already, I may well refuse to believe that even the surface details can be true.

Drama and Ritual

Spoken or written language is not the only vehicle for the telling or the reception of stories. Actions speak far louder than words. The acting out of the events of a story, or watching them acted out by others, fixes them more firmly in the mind than mere telling or hearing – and the inner meanings may likewise be much more firmly imprinted in the unconscious. All these things apply yet more forcefully when the acted story, through frequent repetition, becomes formalized into a ritual, a recognized ceremonial.

The same considerations of truth apply as to the literal story, especially the possibility that fancy or apparent falsity in the surface representation may be accepted, even enthusiastically, so long as the unconscious inner meanings ring true. So with a religious ceremony, for instance, it is entirely possible for the participants to accept and appreciate the spiritual value of what is conveyed without necessarily accepting the literal truth of the imagery in which it is presented.

Myth

I tell my own stories and I re-tell stories which I have adopted. You tell and re-tell yours and others tell and re-tell theirs. Of course, because I am a different person from you and from all of them, with different background and experiences, so the meanings which I find in your stories, or the meanings which you find in mine, on the surface or below it, may never be quite the same as the teller intended, even when sometimes the stories on the surface seem to be the same.

Nevertheless, if the *inner* meanings of our stories are acceptable to the *unconscious* thoughts of both of us then we find that we *share* the story. And when we recognize that the story which we share is to some extent a story about both of us, then we each gain new understanding about the other. And while it is not possible for me ever to know, intellectually, what is in your mind, nor for you to know what is in mine, yet here in the sharing of a story, at levels deeper than ordinary thinking, is the beginning of a way in which we each can know something about the other. That may lead us to share more stories, to learn more of one another, recognize more of our similarities, perhaps eventually become friends.

In this way, through the sharing of stories, groups of people are held together, becoming communities. In every community stories are told and rituals are enacted about the community itself, its members, how it has come to be, and what its hopes and fears are for the future. These stories, with all their inner meanings, shared, told, and understood consciously and unconsciously by all, are the community's *myths*. They are the key to how the community understands itself. They influence everything which the community, and the individuals in it, think and do.

> *The word 'myth' is commonly used nowadays to mean a story which is not true, believed only by people who don't know better. But I am using it here in its proper sense of a story told by a community of people about themselves and* believed, *profoundly, to be a true account of who they are and how they are. So for instance, part of the English myth is the story of the free island people, never invaded by a foreign foe in almost a thousand years. No wonder it is difficult for people sharing that myth even to contemplate sharing a currency, let alone a government, with peoples from across the English (!) Channel.*

For more about the significance of myth in all aspects of life, try Joseph Campbell's Myths to Live By.

Now let us see how these patterns of thought, of metaphor, story, and myth appear in two of the communities to which I belong and which influence me most – that of science and technology and that of religion.

3

Science and Technology

Science

Science is the investigation and measurement of things which we experience, and the hypotheses, theories, and laws which are produced to account for those things.

People observe something, measure it, and imagine possible causes for it. The imaginings take form as a Hypothesis: *possibly* the connections among this set of observations, and a *possible* explanation of them, may be *like this*. Other investigators hear of the hypothesis, think about it, check it experimentally themselves, think of other possibilities, and check them also. In time a majority of those interested and competent in the subject comes to accept one hypothesis as *probably* correct, a reasonable account, as far as can be seen at present, of the things observed. The Hypothesis generally agreed may then be promoted to a Theory, relied upon as true within the limits where it has been tested, to be used, with caution, in further and wider investigations. Yet at the back of people's minds there should always remain the possibility that new information may be found which will show the theory to be wrong, or true only within narrower limits than first supposed. All theories are provisional – potentially falsifiable, as current philosophy has it.

Finally, and rarely, a theory which over a long period has been found to apply under every test which anybody can think of, may come to be called a scientific Law. Still, it can happen that even a law which had been considered firmly established, can be falsified, or at least modified, by new knowledge.

Now all of these scientific accounts and explanations are Stories, with the same properties as any other stories, and with similar implications. A Hypothesis is a story about how things may be; a Theory is a story about how, we think, things probably are; a Law is a story about how, we believe, things really are.

In science *it is essential that all the surface features of every such story must be true.* The material examined, the procedures used, and the data generated must all be capable of being checked by any suitably equipped and competent investigator. So must the starting assumptions, the logic of the suggested connections among the observations, and the proposed explanation of them. That is, the surface details and the surface meaning of the story must all be testable, tested, and found correct. Exaggerations or half-truths are not permitted. Good scientists take care in their experiments and in their thinking to eliminate all possible interferences from outside the precise subject of investigation. The possibilities of external forces, uncontrolled influences, and personal bias must be considered and taken into account from the earliest stage, to ensure that all are excluded, nullified, or suitably allowed for, both in the execution of the experiments and in the story as it is subsequently told.

Nevertheless there are imaginative elements in every scientific experiment. At the very least, the *idea* that it will be worthwhile to do this particular experiment comes most often from a leap of somebody's imagination.

> *I was told that the best experiment is the one designed to answer a single simple question, "Is it like this or is it not?" The imaginative step is in framing the question. If that is done well, making the test and interpreting the result may be relatively simple.*

Every hypothesis and every theory also has its inner meanings.

A 'fruitful' hypothesis suggests new lines of investigation, new ideas to be tested which were not obvious before the hypothesis was imagined. Indeed, 'fruitfulness' is considered to be an essential mark of a good hypothesis.

However, in ordinary routine scientific work in the laboratory, at the desk, or with the computer, the imaginative element and the inner meanings of the story, however significant for further research or for philosophical understanding, will always be secondary to the absolute need for literal and numerical accuracy in the experimental data and the surface details of the story.

Physics – Forces, Actions, and Reactions

We all know, I am sure, about the great shift in scientific thought around the end of the nineteenth century, from the apparent straightforwardness of René Descartes and Isaac Newton to the complexity of Albert Einstein and those who have followed.

> *Nature and Nature's laws lay hid in night.*
> *God said, "Let Newton be!" and all was light.*   *– Alexander Pope*

> *It could not last: the Devil, howling, "Ho!*
> *Let Einstein be!" restored the status quo.*   *– J. C. Squire*

The revolutionary new scientific stories were introduced to correct discrepancies found in the older accounts as they related to the behaviour of the enormously large (galaxies and other solar systems), the minutely small (the insides of atoms), and in some other curious features as well. They now include concepts which previously had been deliberately excluded or never considered:

Uncertainty

With very large numbers you cannot expect to know exact values for every individual but must estimate averages, and the probabilities that any particular individual may be more or less different from the average.

Indeterminacy

It is impossible to measure everything that is there to be

measured. For instance, as Heisenberg's Uncertainty Principle famously states, you cannot determine both the position and the velocity of an atomic particle: the more accurately you know the one the more ignorant you must be about the other.

and *Relativity.*

An observer cannot be independent of the things under observation. Every observation or measurement is *relative* to the observer's position. No two observers in different places can make the same observation, and when they compare their observations they may find them not only different but incompatible. For instance, atoms can be understood to behave *either* as waves *or* as particles. Either interpretation is true, but each excludes the other, and it is not possible to consider them both simultaneously.

I see here three quite fundamental principles. Science may have disclosed them and has certainly accepted them into scientific thinking, but I do not believe them to apply only in some private world of science: they are part of the structure of the whole universe. Let me call them the Principles of Existence.

First, *Everything has its identity, yet everything changes.*

Each component of the universe at each instant is complete in itself, and the total of things in the universe is always the same, yet at every next instant the composition and the arrangement of the components may be different.

Since the first beginning, creation has never been out of nothing, always out of something already there. Existing bits have come together in new combinations, developed into new possibilities.

So matter was first formed out of energy; everything which is in the universe now has come about and operates through transformations of the energy and matter which were there before it.

> *First Law of Thermodynamics: Heat and mechanical work are interconvertible.*

Secondly, *Every change has a cost.*

You get nothing for nothing.

No change happens 'by itself', only through the conversion of something else – which itself is changed in the process. Perpetual motion of an isolated body is impossible; energy must be supplied from somewhere. You can't heat anything without burning something else.

> *Second Law of Thermodynamics: Heat cannot be transferred from a colder to a hotter body by any continuous, self-sustaining process.*

Thirdly, *Order and freedom come together.*

Everything in the universe at any given instant is both unique, with its own degree of freedom of action, and unavoidably connected with other things in more or less complex systems or groups. Yet the existence of the systems imposes limits on the freedom of the individual components. Absolute order and absolute freedom are equally impossible; the relationship between the free individual and the ordered system is always one of some tension and some uncertainty.

> *Third Law of Thermodynamics: The absolute zero of temperature [0 K or –273.16 °C, where everything is frozen and nothing moves] can never be attained.*

Everything that is works by these principles; the principles themselves do not change.

In earlier times, when extraordinary and inexplicable things happened, people called them miracles. They said that they must be caused by gods who had power to change the ordinary rules, interfering with events for reasons of their own. Now I don't believe in miracles like that. If anything unexpected happens I expect there to be reasons, within these basic principles, and I am confident that they will be found if we look hard enough.

Chemistry and Biochemistry – Change and Growth

Chemists study how the particles described by physicists come together in more or less complex groupings to form new substances with new properties, and how those substances may interact, change, and disappear. Biochemists study the processes as they occur in living things.

As with Physics, the same Principles of Existence apply:

Everything has its identity, yet everything changes.

The chemical elements, each with its own existence and its own properties, were formed in turn from pure hydrogen. The hard rocks of mountains turn slowly into agricultural land. Plants take mineral salts from the land and carbon dioxide from the air and convert them into their own vegetable substance.

Every change has a cost.

Every chemical change involves energy, either paid in to enable the formation of more complex or more stable substances, or given out as the structure of some substance is decomposed. The energy 'paid in' when a complex system (fuel oil, for instance) was first formed is made available when the system is broken down later (for instance, on burning it to heat my living room). And on laboratory walls you may sometimes see the beautiful (I think) diagrams of biological pathways: the complex interlinking patterns of chemical reactions, by which all the substances of living bodies are built up from the materials and the energy contained in other substances also present there.

Order and freedom come together.

In all the fantastic complexity of the world there is a remarkable degree of order. There are some astonishingly simple chemical and biochemical regularities: the same DNA-RNA system in principle governs the structure and the reproduction of all living things. The same DNA is to be found in every cell of my body. In every living creature the same ATP-ADP system converts the chemical energy from carbohydrates into the working energy which the creature needs. The piston movement of myosin and actin molecules is the universal engine which converts that energy into action, from the bending of your arm to the turning of a flower towards the sun.

Yet the order is always accompanied by freedom, by some disorder as the components vibrate, oscillate, or move around in random fashion. The patterns of inheritance in living things undergo occasional unpredictable changes or mutations as the strands of DNA move about while reproducing themselves.

(The methods of mathematical statistics are used to describe the extent and some of the implications of the variability, the degrees of freedom which are to be found in every ordered group of molecules, objects, creatures, or people.)

Beyond Science

There are many who claim that science and the scientific method are capable unaided of uncovering all that we ever need to know about our world. But there are some, myself included, who believe that there exist realities which science can never comprehend nor discover. In the 1960s some of the physicists studying the strange world of sub-atomic particles became convinced, through *that* scientific experience, that there must be realities beyond the ones they could measure or envisage or predict. They were only indirectly suggested by their experimental results, yet accessible through processes beyond those of ordinary logic and experiment. They tell *scientific* stories about *spiritual* realities, to be encountered by those who seek to do so, beyond the facts and interpretations of 'normal' science.

> *Fritjof Capra's* The Tao of Physics *contributes to "an awareness of a profound harmony between the world view of science and the mystical tradition", says the cover of my copy. In a different way Douglas Hofstadter in* Gödel, Escher, Bach *("in the spirit of Lewis Carroll", as he puts it), explores the profound harmony between Kurt Gödel's Theorem (that there exist true mathematical statements which cannot be mathematically proved), and M.C. Escher's drawings of impossible objects, J. S. Bach's music, and much else.*

Technology

Technology is the art of making things, and making things happen.

Today there is a lot of talk about 'high' technology – electronic information transfer, micro-surgery, gene manipulation, and the like. But the ancient 'low' technologies, which used to be called 'crafts' – making food, clothing, buildings, tools, and so on – are not only still around, they represent a far greater proportion of most people's activities than the 'high' technologies do. Despite the enormous attention paid in our society to the newer and higher technologies, and the fears which some of them appear to generate, it is the lower technologies that we all depend on for almost all the necessities of life, and which, by and large, we trust to supply them. Still, what follows should refer to all kinds of technology, high and low, newer and older.

Technologists are people who understand scientifically *how* the technology works. They know, and can tell and act, both craft stories and scientific stories, each in the light of the other. With that understanding they can, when necessary, seek and find ways to modify, adapt, or extend an existing technology, or get it to work more reliably or more consistently. Then they can write the instructions, recipes, and formulae which will simply need to be followed carefully, usually by others, to produce satisfactory results in the future.

For to exercise a craft or to *do* technology you don't have to *be* a technologist. You don't have to understand how the technology works, you don't need to know the science. You only need to know *what to do* and *how to do it.* You just follow the instructions which the technologist – or the tradition – has given you. The converse of this is also true. A scientist or even a technologist, with excellent knowledge of *how* a process works, need not be able personally to work it very well.

There is a closely similar relationship between education (opening minds to *think* and to *understand* things) and training (teaching people to *do* things). I came to appreciate this during my service as an Education Officer in the RAF. There I learned the military method of training which embodies all that I see in the practice of technology:

- specify exactly what it is that you want done and the abilities which a person will need to be able to be trained to do it;

- describe the task as clearly and simply as possible in a written manual;
- select people with the necessary abilities;
- tell them exactly what is in the manual, demonstrate it, and make them rehearse it as often as necessary until they can do it by themselves;
- test them to confirm that they can do it unaided;
- reward them and certify their new competence with badges, promotion or whatever.

The system is designed to be positive and efficient. It builds upon strength to produce greater strength. It can and does identify failures, but attempts to do so as early as possible so as to waste the minimum of effort. Any failure to complete training successfully is considered first to be due to some error in the system (faulty initial selection of the trainees, faulty design of the manual or the training course, or some other change in circumstances), none of which need be taken as defects in the trainee.

So it is not necessary either in technology or in training for everybody to know everything in order to get things done properly. I see this as an example of another general principle, widely applicable, maybe even universally. Let me call it the Incompleteness Principle, to be set alongside the three already considered:

Nobody can do everything or know everything, but it is not necessary that they should.

Now, to be more specific:

Food Science and Technology

I have spent my life, by choice, in and around the food industry, working with its science, its technology, and its people.

My livelihood, the quality of my life, and those of my family too, are intimately bound up with my understanding of food science and my practice of food technology. The income which has supported me and my family in moderate comfort, and continues to do so in retirement, and the other enrichments of my life, all depend, directly, upon them.

This is so not only for my life. Whatever else may matter to the rest of humanity, its life cannot exist at all without food. The lives of multitudes of people depend directly on the food which I and many companions prepare for them.

> *Some people are surprised to discover how large is the modern food industry and how many people work in it. In older times, we know that almost everybody was involved for almost all of their 'working' hours in hunting, gathering, harvesting, preparing, and preserving food. Now that all our occupations have become specialized we tend to forget how much effort is still required to keep us all, and how much has to be provided by the specialists in other tasks than our own.*

> *Food manufacture, not including retailing the food in shops and supermarkets, employs some half a million people. It is the largest single manufacturing industry in the UK, at 15 per cent by value of manufacturing output, followed closely only by electrical goods at 12 per cent. Correspondingly, more of our domestic spending (17 per cent) goes on food than on housing, motoring, leisure, or anything else. (Figures from the* Annual Digest of Statistics, *HMSO, 1994, 1999.)*

Now if I want to say anything about the ways that I think, the things that I believe, about religious practice, or anything else, all must be consistent with everything that I know and trust about food, the making of food, and the providing of food. My understanding of science and technology, and their place in the whole scheme of existence, precedes my religious understanding of any of these things.

First let me point out how the universal Principles of Existence and the Incompleteness Principle apply in every aspect of my work, and that of my colleagues, in food science and technology.

Everything has its identity, yet everything changes:
- the food industry is there, and has been for ages, growing out of domestic crafts, doing essentially the same things yet changing continuously in scope and in methods;
- the raw materials used have also 'always' been there, yet

their form, composition, locations, methods of collection
likewise change slowly and continuously;
- the crafts and the modern industry are themselves instruments
of change as they transform raw materials into edible food;
- food itself is only one vital stage in the flow of all existence
on the earth, of the conversions from rocks to soil, from
plants to animals, from food to human beings.

Every change has a cost:
- every benefit from the food we eat comes with costs in
human effort (in our society measured mostly in money);
- there are other less obvious costs: if you convert grains of
wheat into bread for food you cannot have that wheat for
next year's seed;
- every food for humans, vegetable and animal alike, comes at
the cost of the life which was in the vegetables and the animals before;
- it is difficult to measure and apportion all the costs which
are raised by the fears which people have about, for
instance, a BSE epidemic and the possible risks of contract-
ing new-variant Creutzfeldt-Jacob disease.

Order and freedom come together:
- the food industry says that it intends to give maximum freedom of choice to consumers, and consumers say that their
freedom of choice is restricted to what the industry makes
available: both may be correct;
- in such things as the setting of nutritional standards, the
choosing of diets, or the making of legal regulations, there
is always tension and uncertainty between the steps which it
may be practical to take and the fact that no general deci-
sion 'for the best' can ever be exactly right for all the mar-
ginal or exceptional cases;
- similarly at a deeper, more technical level, any such decisions which depend on information about the composition
of the foods in question must be subject to more or less
unpredictable errors due to natural variations among
different samples of the food.

Incompleteness, Relativity and Uncertainty apply throughout:

- in any factory the staff, the technologists, and the scientists undertake their different tasks in the whole process as well as they are able, but never completely perfectly, for all are incomplete and fallible;
- while each operation in a whole chain of events may be dealt with, in detail and reasonably carefully and competently, by particular persons or groups or systems, those dedicated people and systems need have little or no knowledge or competence in any of the other operations upon which they depend or which depend upon them;
- with co-operation among the people in a well organized system such as a factory, production line, or laboratory, the work as a whole can be done better than by any of the individuals alone, but again never quite perfectly, for even co-operative systems are incomplete and fallible;
- when the food is made, as well as may be, no single item of it can ever be completely satisfactory for all the needs, or the wishes, of every individual consumer.

Other Occupations

I have tried to describe how the general principles which I believe to apply to all of existence, can be seen to apply consistently and in fine detail throughout the world of food manufacture. Perhaps I have taken a certain risk of baffling, even upsetting, some readers who do not share my interest in that world, certainly not any close knowledge of it. But I believe that those general principles apply in every human activity, and I trust that even if your interests and your experience are quite different from mine, if you look at them closely you too will find that the very same principles apply there, and at every point.

Now let us turn to religious ways of seeing and expressing these things which I believe are there to be seen, everywhere, by religious and non-religious alike.

4

Religion

Religious Stories

The difference between science and religion, it has been said, is that science deals with 'how' questions, religion with 'why' questions. Or, put another way, science deals with the 'natural' things which can be measured, can be known, and may be presumed to exist, whilst religion deals with 'supernatural' things which cannot be measured or known, and which, ultimately, may not even exist in any 'natural' sense.

From the earliest human times people must have asked both 'how' and 'why' questions. The first of the 'how' questions will have included most of the ones of everyday practical experience – how to find food, get shelter, make garments, control fire – and those about the causes of some things outside human control – sunsets and storms, volcanoes and earthquakes, the growth and the deaths of plants and animals and people. 'How' and 'why' came mixed together as human beings pondered their inner feelings of pleasure and misery about things which happened, of hope and fear about things which might happen. And there must always have been the deepest and most difficult questions of all: "*Why* is life like this? What is it all *for*? Where do I come from and where am I going?"

From the earliest times also, people must have known that there were things which they did not know about. There were things in the natural world around them which they could not account for, and therefore did not 'know'. And I am sure that there was, as I know there is in me, the sense of mystery provoked by their feelings, their emotions, and maybe by some of their experience too, *about* things which happen, by the sense that there is more to life than our own experience of it.

At first there was not enough knowledge around to answer more than a very few of even the 'how' questions. But the questions seemed important and human curiosity, as always, wanted answers. So people did what intelligent people always do: they used their imagination and composed stories to account for what could not be accounted for otherwise. So do scientists when faced with apparent facts lacking explanation: they imagine a hypothesis.

At first nearly everything in the natural world had to be accounted for in such stories. The unknown forces which caused the sun and the moon and the stars to behave as they were seen to do, which caused thunder and hailstones and hosts of other things, were imagined as gods possessing the necessary supernatural powers to cause the things which were so obviously happening. Thus were formed the earliest animistic religions, some of which have persisted in parts of the world at least until very recently. Then came the more developed religions of the Egyptians, Babylonians, Aztecs, Minoans, and every other ancient civilization that we know about, followed in their turn by the great religions of today – Hindu, Buddhist, Confucian, Muslim, Jewish, Christian. All have been formed in essentially the same way, to give intelligent, imagined accounts of things which otherwise would remain inexplicable. (Of course, not everything in their accounts had to be imaginary. For instance, as historical records began to be written, stories of significant historical events and people were also incorporated.)

> *Every religion is a set of stories composed, developed, told, and enacted by the people of a particular society to account for things otherwise inexplicable. They were the best stories imaginable by those people, in their time and their circumstances, with whatever knowledge and whatever beliefs, true or false, as were commonly held at the time.*

Exactly the same is said, please note, of the theories and laws of science. They are the best available explanations in current circumstances, of information otherwise unexplainable.

Like every story, the religious stories have limitations: the Incompleteness Principle applies (the stories cannot possibly see or tell all that there is to be seen and told, only those parts which were seen from the standpoint of those who first told or later modified them). And they are conditioned and constrained by the actual knowledge, experience, and history of their composers.

So, because every religious story is both conditioned by circumstances and inevitably incomplete, it should cause no surprise to find that different stories are told and different religions exist, side by side in different communities, even among close neighbours.

Belief and Practice

Religion everywhere is marked by the things that people *do*, in rituals and ceremonies, public and private. The rituals, and the stories told and enacted within them, are intended to express and to cultivate the beliefs of people about spiritual matters. In every religion stories are told about the gods who are believed to cause good and bad things to happen, and about the ways which people should follow to maximize the good things. Rituals are performed in the hope that good may follow, harm be avoided, and sometimes even that the apparent course of nature may be turned in people's favour.

When we speak of 'religion' this is what we generally mean: the visible expressions of a community's beliefs, the complex of stories told and enacted by the community about itself.

But the correspondence between religious practice and the beliefs which gave rise to the practice is not always close. Positively, I find that sometimes when I experience or participate in a religious ceremony – especially one in which others are engaged with fervour – though I may have little thought about the meaning of what is going on, or even have marked mental reservations about it, I can feel that my spirit is engaged and in some way enriched. Of course this is one of the objects of the ceremony. Negatively, there are occasions when I can neither see nor feel much connection between the particular religious ceremony and things which I believe to be practically or spiritually true. This may mean that I am in need of instruction or of spiritual awakening, but it might also mean that the religious practice which I observe is in some way deficient or even false.

Religious and Scientific Truth

Pontius Pilate was not the first or the last to ask, "What is truth?"

No story which is told by any incomplete, fallible human person or society about anything else, can ever be a completely true account of that thing. It can be no more than a fair description of those features of it which came to the mind of the composer of the story. Like any metaphor, the story may be true and false at the same time, and at the very least, whatever reality the story is supposed to be *about* is likely to be much greater than the story is able to tell.

If a religious story, like a scientific one, is to serve its purpose as an explanation and therefore as an inspiration and guide for future activity, and if it is to continue to be told for that purpose, it must first be *believable* by those who hear it. But the grounds for belief, the source of the *truth* of the story, are different in the two cases.

> *In science it is essential that the* surface features *of every story, hypothesis, or theory must be true. What matters for a religious story is that the* inner *meanings must be* felt *to be true.*

The surface details may or may not be literally true, may even be clearly fanciful, as long as the inner meanings are true to the hearers' own unconscious knowledge and understanding. Indeed, religious stories are most often rejected by people who, finding the surface details incredible, refuse to go further and so fail to engage with the hidden meanings below the surface.

Note how rich in inner meanings are all the longest standing stories of gods and their superhuman activities. The Myths of the Greek gods, and many others, are memorable and satisfying as stories, in the same way as the fairy stories. Yet however fanciful we may nowadays think their form and their superficial meanings to be, we go on telling the same stories in books and plays and films, and we continue to be affected by their inner truths, their accounts of some of the deepest human feelings.

Very many of the old religious stories were first told as answers to 'how' questions and have now been superseded, for us, by more believable scientific accounts. Still, some of the stories continue to be told even where their form and surface details are in conflict with the scientific accounts which we take for granted in practical life. Where this happens it may sometimes be because the *point* of the religious story is still believed to be true, but must always be because the *inner meanings* continue to accord with unconscious thoughts and feelings which are much the same in people now as when the stories were first told.

Natural and Supernatural

I know there are people who say that there is no such thing as 'supernatural'; 'natural' is all that there is. Sooner or later, those people say, the human race will know and understand all that there is to know, or at least enough to satisfy human curiosity: witness how fast our knowledge is already advancing. So, they say, the only answer to a 'why' question is 'because (full stop)'. Things are the way they are and that is all that needs be said.

When people *say* that, I receive it as what they *believe*. But I find that belief inadequate. Nobody can *know* whether or not there is a supernatural (by definition, something beyond what is natural for us to know), but I see no reason to say that therefore it is impossible. On the contrary, I choose to believe not only that it is possible, but also that some of our human experience (certainly, some of mine) raises the possibility to a high probability, close to a certainty. So I believe, though like everybody else I cannot *know* it, never prove it.

Yet I must remember that the I who holds that belief about a 'supernatural' am myself a 'natural' human being. Every belief that I hold, I hold in my human mind. I don't know who first said that all religions are human creations, or that all gods are psychological projections of human fears and hopes, but I see an important truth in the statements. It is not that God is 'only' a projection, a wish-fulfilment, a human creation, as I hear some people say. But whilst I can never *know* whether an independent God exists or not, I do think *about* God, or the possibility of God; and the only way I can do *that*, in my human mind, is to work with what my mind *imagines*, with mental, human *images*.

I can think about God only through images.

All the modern religions are quite explicit about this. No living person may see God face to face, they tell; anybody who does will die. Moses, so one story goes, was exceptionally favoured with the promise that he might see God, but in the event all that he managed was a glimpse of God's back.

It was not always so. The Greek Myths tell of gods and humans who met and had intercourse together. The story is told of the Hebrew Jacob, long before Moses, wrestling all night with someone who might have been God (only he wouldn't say).

Furthermore, the Second Commandment of the Hebrews insists that only God is to be worshipped, not any image made by people. Graham Shaw argues the same point in the book whose title proclaims it, *God in Our Hands*.

It is the images which are human creations, not God. Every humanly created image, inevitably, is incomplete, imperfect, fallible.

So, after all that, I find that I should do two things. I must continue to check that my religious beliefs agree with the other things that I *do* know, in all the ways that I have said, and I must be wary when they do not. That done, I can make the 'leap of faith' and *commit* myself, by a positive act of my own will, to the belief that there is an unknowable something which I am willing to call 'God'. Then I may go on to believe certain things about that God.

Commitment and Conviction

Many of my religious friends say that religious truth cannot be reached by systematic thinking, but only by *revelation*. I think they mean that for them the truth of a religious story or statement was shown to them as a complete whole, often 'in a flash', by something or someone outside ordinary experience (usually they say 'it came from God'), and it seems that they then do not feel a need for any further rational checking of any part of the story. Their commitment to belief in the story seems to be not from deliberate

34 HOW I THINK

choice among alternatives as I have been describing for myself,
but rather by the acceptance of a single option.

I think I understand what these people say, and I have no
reason to doubt that this is how it is with them. But it has not been
like that with me. I do know that I have not thought my own way
unaided into everything which I now believe, nor followed only
the thoughts of others. Much of what I believe has indeed 'come
to me', has been revealed, from sources outside me. But the
revelations did not come in a single convincing moment, nor even
in several lesser ones, and they were never so strong as to over-
whelm all previous uncertainties.

> *Dag Hammarskjöld's words (in* Markings*) describe my state most
> nearly: "Once I answered Yes to Someone – or Something. And from
> that hour I was certain that existence is meaningful and that, therefore,
> my life in self-surrender, has a goal."*

I do have one observation. When a belief is formed in that way,
when a person has accepted the belief and committed themselves
to it without checking that it is consistent with everything else
which the mind knows and believes, then the commitment can
readily become a *conviction* that the *whole story*, form, surface
details, point and all, is *the* Truth. It then seems to be difficult or
even impossible for the believer to consider any other account,
sometimes even any minor variant of the story which has been
accepted, for fear that the whole belief will be destroyed. For then
not only an abstract belief, an idea, is challenged, but also the
believer's personal commitment to that belief. To agree that an
idea may be wrong is much less difficult than to admit that one
was wrong to have committed oneself to it.

For then you must face the argument: "I *chose* to believe *that*, I
committed myself to it because I had been convinced it was right. Was
I wrong on such an important matter? Do I dare to tell myself now
that the I who has to make all the decisions of my life, couldn't get
that one right? That I shouldn't ever trust myself again?"

I believe that it is such a *fear of change to one's convictions* which is
the main reason that so many people get upset by any suggestions

of alternatives to their accustomed religious beliefs or practices.

I believe too that the same process operates in other areas besides the religious, and in all of us to some extent. I know that I react strongly against and try to avoid discussing or even thinking about certain things. They are things which I know are important, which strongly affect me, whose causes and whose power lie largely beyond my understanding or control.

I do hold strong beliefs about them, most of which I suspect 'came to me' once from somewhere outside, most of which I have never fully tested, and many of which are now unconscious. And I observe in other people similar embarrassment and unwillingness when the same subjects are raised.

Most often, these are the great universal subjects of sex and politics, as well as religion. There are also my direct reactions to the physical presence of other people, where we all have powerful feelings and urges, many of them unacknowledged or repressed. Not least are relationships among groups of people, where events are determined in very complex ways, where my own influence is minute, yet where I and others hold strong but divergent views, to which we have become committed, about what *ought* to be done.

It is no wonder therefore that these are the topics usually to be avoided in polite conversation, for fear that any of our commitments or our unconscious convictions might be upset. It is no wonder either that there is so much difficulty in public life, so much incomprehension and conflict among us all, when all our relationships with one another lie precisely within one or more of those same unmentionable areas.

Christianity

The stories of the Christian religion are those found in the Bible, expanded by creeds and supplementary documents such as confessions, articles of religion, and papal statements.

For those who may not be familiar with the field, a brief note:

> *Scholars of the Bible over the last century and a half have shown how complex a creation is that collection of books. They were written and*

compiled at various times, edited and re-edited by different people and groups to bring out different understandings, or to make different religious or political points.

In the Hebrew Scriptures (the Christian Old Testament) the scholars have distinguished Myths (many with close parallels to the Myths of neighbouring peoples) from historical accounts (as one-sided and as liable to exaggeration and omission as every other history), legends about heroes, rules of religious observance, and customary laws of society. They have shown how all these accounts were formed, and sometimes later altered, at particular times in particular situations, by minds conditioned by the knowledge and the assumptions of their times, and how they may give us clues about the culture and beliefs of those times. Behind all this we can also begin to see how people's understanding of God developed through those experiences. For instance, the views of God of prophets such as Amos or Hosea are very different from those expressed by the writers and compilers of Genesis.

In the New Testament are the four Gospels (theologically interpreted accounts of the life, death and resurrection of Jesus), the Acts of the Apostles (an account of the early growth of the Christian Church), letters written by Paul and others, and the dream-like Revelation of St John. Similar critical analysis has been applied to these books also, so that we can now understand much about the circumstances in which each account was written, its intended readership, and some of the distinctive religious points which individual writers were trying to make.

The supplementary statements – creeds, confessions, and the like – represent further developments, found necessary as new questions were asked about some of the implications of earlier assertions. So the Apostles' Creed reached its present form in the late fourth century, the Nicene Creed in the fifth. Of course, the concepts they had to deal with, and the thought forms in which they expressed them, are those of their time, and not all of them are easy to follow now.

Today, some of the concepts and expressions used (for instance, phrases in the creeds about the substance of God or the conception of Jesus) may be less than helpful. Yet I believe that in all of these stories there are *inner truths*, as true now as when the accounts were composed, and many of the stories are still good vehicles for telling those truths.

So, for myself, I am prepared to read and tell most of them as they are given, though wherever it is possible I like to indicate that it is not essential to believe that every surface detail must be literally true. As I sometimes put it in preaching or in discussion of the biblical accounts, scholars have their doubts whether things *did* happen just like that, then, but I know that the same things *do* happen, like that, now.

In the next chapters I shall consider some of those inner truths of the Christian story and also some of the traditional expressions, the surface details of some versions of the story, which I believe can be interpreted both meaningfully and fully consistently with a scientific understanding

Other Religions

There are of course many stories told and enacted by people in other branches of the Christian Church than mine and in other faiths. I am aware of some of the differences among them.

I know too that people of those other faiths and denominations all say that their religious stories are true, and at the level of their inner meanings I do not disagree. All faiths, including mine, are partial, incomplete attempts to describe and to communicate with the same Reality which is beyond any of us to understand completely. All are conditioned by, and all have special insights from, their own experience and history. I do not believe any one to be 'better' than any other, except in the limited sense that perhaps one way of looking might be able to see a greater proportion of the whole Reality than another. Perhaps that is the case with the version of Christianity which I accept. Whether that is so or not I see no reason to change my version for any other. But neither do I think that any honest follower of another religion need be less in contact with the deeper truths of life than I am, nor understand them less, nor be less well placed in his journey towards them.

There is of course the practical problem that almost every religious group appears to have at least some members who do say that their religion is the only true one, that all the others are false. Where two such groups come into contact, conflict is inevitable, and as long as protagonists on either side are convinced of their own version of truth and committed to proclaiming it, then the conflict is almost impossible to resolve.

Part 2:
What I believe

❖❖❖❖❖❖❖❖❖❖❖❖❖❖❖❖

5

God as Spirit

All religions recognize that whatever else God may be, God is Spirit.

Christian doctrine has much to say about the Holy Spirit, though not usually as the first of the things to be considered. However I think it helpful to start here.

My Spirit

I believe that there is a spirit or a soul in me, along with my body and my mind, but not the same as either. In my spirit I recognize such things as truth, beauty, goodness, and love, and their opposites, falsehood, ugliness, evil, and hate. In my spirit I *know* what they *are*, sometimes as things which my mind can think about, sometimes as emotions which my mind can hardly manage. I don't know *how* my spirit knows these things, but I am sure that it does.

Yes, I am aware that some people say that these things are purely mental and physical effects, and that there is no need to suppose any 'spirit' to explain them. But I don't find that adequate. I do *encounter* music, poetry, smiling, and good food and wine through my physical senses, and my mind can consciously think *about* them; but the *beauty* of them, the *goodness* of them, my feelings about them, and the uplifting effect which they can have on me – I don't believe that I can account for those as 'purely mental and physical'.

I cannot say where that spirit may be located, but I suspect that much of its activity takes place in my unconscious. Its reflections then seem to find their way from there into conscious thought and into bodily behaviour. Dreams seem to work in a similar way, as they try to tell me truths which my unconscious knows but my conscious mind hasn't recognized.

I know that I can concentrate on one aspect of myself at a time, so that sometimes (nearly all the time?) I am mostly acting and reacting physically, sometimes I am mostly thinking mentally. There are other times when body and mind are still, when my spirit can reflect on whatever it will. Sometimes those states may occur together, sometimes I may deliberately encourage one or more of them. Sometimes (mostly?) it does not seem that my spirit does anything, that anything is happening there, yet at other times I become very conscious of some of its effects. For instance, I know that some kinds of music have deep effects upon me. Sometimes I think about the music when I am listening, often I don't, and sometimes I don't even seem to be listening, but I am sure the effects are there, in my spirit.

My spirit, whatever it 'really' is, exists on the edges of my physical and mental capacities, in contact with them, but also in some sense beyond them. And if there are other things which 'really' do exist, but beyond my human capacity to see or measure or understand, then it seems to me that the best way, perhaps the only way, to know anything about them must be through my spirit.

The Spirit Beyond Me

I believe that there is *a* Spirit of the whole universe, greater than all my experience or that of anybody else. I can't prove it, of course, but the belief fits consistently with the other things which I know and believe to be true.

If my spirit reflects for instance on what is good, I believe that there is such a thing as goodness for it to reflect upon, beyond me and independent of me. I also believe that the goodness which I know is itself part of some greater Goodness which is universally Good. I know that I am incomplete and fallible, that I cannot possibly see enough or know enough, even of the good things which matter, so that my thoughts and my actions can never themselves be completely good; nevertheless Goodness exists and I know it. So I also believe about truth, beauty, love, and all the other things of the spirit.

This universal Spirit influences my spirit, I believe, strongly and intimately, just as the universal gravitational force influences my body. Its influence from beyond me joins that of the spirit within me. Just as my body is nourished and its fabric maintained by the food within me which previously was outside me, so my spirit, I am sure, feeds upon and is nourished by the Spirit which is both beyond and within me.

The Spirit of Science

I see that Spirit plainly in all the workings of science. It is the atmosphere, the ethos in which science is conducted, and in which scientists conduct themselves. Its properties, behaviour, and activities are the same in the world of science as everywhere else.

Scientists expect a good theory, formula, or experimental design to be *elegant* – or beautiful. I can recognize and enjoy the elegance, and I know that others in the science community also recognize, enjoy, and seek it.

I *love* the science which I know and the technology which I practise. I care about them; I feel encouraged and sustained through that caring, not just by the practical results. I hear, read, and see instances of the respect and attention – that is, the love – paid by others to the science and the technology within which they work.

We recognize that Spirit personally and with our emotions, but there are also impersonal, unemotional realities upon which all science depends. There are the *rules* of arithmetic, the *principles* of logic, and the *laws* of physics and chemistry which the whole physical universe follows. None of these was created or invented by any person. They have been *discovered*. They were there already, waiting to be discovered; maybe there are more, still waiting. Meanwhile, discovered or not, they are *there*, helpful, effective, and completely reliable – just as religious people say of the Spirit of God.

There is mystery about the source of all these things. Recognition or understanding of them so often comes unconsciously, bypassing logical thought. Answers to technical questions have 'come to me' when I thought I was not thinking about them at all;

I know that others say the same. There is the story, well known among chemists, of Kekulé who dreamed of a snake biting its tail and 'saw' the molecular structure of benzene.

This way of discovering truth – Truth which was true before we discovered it – is as real and as effective as the logical way or the practical experimental way. It is a spiritual way, even if some do not care to call it so.

The Spirit of Food Science and Technology

The same Spirit operates everywhere, I believe, even in solemn institutions. The Institute of Food Science and Technology of the United Kingdom (IFST), the independent qualifying body for my profession, states its primary objectives as:

– to serve the public interest by furthering the application of science and technology to all relevant aspects of the supply of safe, wholesome, nutritious, and attractive food, nationally and internationally;

– to advance the standing of food science and technology, both as a subject and as a profession;

– to assist members in their career and personal development within the profession of food science and technology;

– to uphold professional standards of competence and integrity.

What are these but statements of the *spirit* in which the Institute expects to conduct itself, and expects its members to conduct themselves? I am happy to live and to work in that spirit, and more than happy to know that it is what my colleagues declare.

Take a single example of that Spirit of beauty, of elegance, of truth, from laboratory experience. How shall I describe the satisfaction which my spirit feels when I find, again and again, in work which I have done myself, and even more in work done by assistants, the sheer reliability of it all, when for instance, separate chemical analyses of the moisture, protein, fat, carbohydrate, and ash contents of a food add up together to 100 per cent, with experimental errors well under one per cent?

God the Spirit

The Holy Spirit of Christians, the Great Spirit of the Red Indians, the Nirvana of Buddhists, are all expressions of that same universal Spirit. The Buddhist and Hindu religions operate explicitly on the spiritual level. Hindus tell of a great number of individual gods, and appear to Western eyes to be quite relaxed both about the rituals of worship and about doctrine (what ought to be believed), but they take immense care over the spiritual quality of their worship. Buddhists appear to have no particular beliefs in any gods but they insist on the necessity of spiritual means of directing human life, along the Eightfold Path, towards Nirvana, the delightful spiritual existence which they hope for beyond this life.

Christianity, Judaism, and Islam, with their common belief in only one God, all likewise understand well that the spiritual reality of that God can be approached by people only through spiritual means, and they cultivate methods for doing so. So they encourage and assist people to make contact with the Spirit of God though prayer and meditation, and in ceremonies in which appointed ministers are charged to facilitate that contact on behalf of the others present. Words, music and song, the form and decoration of buildings, and the movements of people are all designed especially to direct the thoughts and the feelings of the worshippers in spiritual ways.

I believe that making and fostering spiritual contact with the Spirit of God is an essential purpose and function of every religion.

> *"God is Spirit and those who worship God must worship in spirit and in truth."* — *John 4:24*

Prayer

Now I believe that it is the same Spirit which underlies and is involved in every activity in the universe, including all the activities of science and of technology, and which is to be encountered and appreciated by people in every activity in exactly similar ways. So in my own work, for instance, I encounter the Spirit, the truth which underlies it all, in all the stories and the rituals of laboratory experiments, of food production processes, of management, and of quality assurance. And the encounters are fostered as I try to keep my spirit open to the universal Spirit, the Spirit of God.

The opening of one's own spirit to the Spirit of God is what in the religious world is called prayer. That is not just asking for things which I would like to happen, or sudden exclamations of need, though these may sometimes be important. More significant is the recognition that I may know much more than my conscious mind thinks it knows. Through my spirit I can get in touch with truths which my spirit knows, truths in my unconscious mind, and the Truth which is all around me, all only waiting to be appreciated. Then, in touch with the universal Spirit, I may indeed know sufficient to be able to choose wisely in the practical affairs of life.

So for instance, if I begin the day with five minutes of quiet contemplation of my List of Things to Do (as I discovered long ago was the practice of several of the bosses whom I most respected), allowing them to fall into an order of priority, pondering where I may need help and what I shall have to leave to others – an ordinary management task – what is that but my morning prayer, a deliberate attempt to align myself with the spirit in which my day is to be conducted?

The scientist's daydreams, the poet's musings, work in the same ways. All these can lead to a deeper understanding of Truth, to the discovery of realities which would not be reached by logical thought alone.

6

God and Creation

This is where religious discussions most often seem to start: not, as in the last chapter, with "How do I encounter God?" but with "What is God supposed to *do*?", or the secondary question "What must God be *like*, to do such things?" These are proper questions too.

God

I believe that there is a creative force which 'caused the universe to begin' from some point when there was nothing there, nor any space for anything to be 'in' nor any time for anything to be 'before'. That force, that Ground of Being as some have called it, set the universe going and set the rules by which it has functioned ever since. The rules apply universally, are open enough to allow all the possibilities of development and growth of the created universe, including degrees of freedom and variability in the components created under them, but are themselves invariable.

This of course is the story as Big Bang theory tells it. At first there was only Energy (whatever that is), from which all else has followed. It is not a new story. John began his Gospel by quoting from Greek philosophers of his time, "In the beginnig was the Word..." and he went on, "and the Word was God..."

I believe that such a force 'really' exists. It is not the same as the universe itself, nor any part of the universe. Nor is it Nothing, though in the beginning there was nothing else. Yet neither is it separate from the created universe, rather it permeates every detail of the existence and activity of the universe.

I am willing to call such a force God. But if I ask myself what such a God might be *like*, I have to reply that I believe the question can never be properly answered by a human mind. St Anselm's twelfth-century definition as "that than which nothing greater can be thought" feels right to me. The God that is beyond all human thought, but that does exist as Spirit, cannot be known by me directly through my mind, only through my spirit, through parts of me which lie beyond thought – or perhaps indirectly by my mind when my mind is empty, or filled only with negatives. This is God seen in the *via negativa*, the negative way, as that which God is not, in the 'dark night of the soul' from which God is absent.

Yet in my mind I can *imagine* what God *may* be like. If I want to think about God at all, or any possibility of God, that is what I shall have to do. So also will anybody else. Of course, as I have said, that is what all religions do and all that any religion can do. They make *human* attempts to understand what God *may* be like; they make *images*, with the dangers which that entails, they tell stories, and they draw conclusions about how humans should respond. Still, all religious images and stories have their inner meanings, giving glimpses, more or less true, of the realities which they try to describe.

The Existence of God

There are many who say, as Laplace the mathematician and astronomer said when Napoleon asked where was God in his scheme of things, "Sire, I have no need of that hypothesis."

But I say that I do believe in God. I find the hypothesis, like every good hypothesis, to be a successful explanation of many other things and a fruitful source of new insights. At the same time I know, with Laplace, that I do not *need* the hypothesis for all of the purposes for which many of *his* contemporaries considered it essential – and some of *my* contemporaries still seem to do.

Some modern or post-modern philosophers and theologians – Don Cupitt is probably the most prominent example – say something else about the existence of God. They may agree to give the name 'God' to the fundamental force of the universe, whatever it is, but they go on to insist that the name should not be taken to imply that there is anything 'really' there. God, they say, is 'non-real'. Rowan Williams says (in his Introduction to Colin Crowder's

God and Reality) that this is not a question about whether God exists but rather about the *manner* of God's existence. I think that is true: God exists but God's existence is not *like* anything which we can describe as 'real'.

Non-real things do exist. Mathematicians have long imagined the square root of minus one, a mathematical quantity which is logically impossible; they call it a 'surd', an absurd, irrational or non-real thing. Yet it does exist in mathematicians' minds and on the pages of school textbooks. It is freely employed, along with the equally puzzling concept of fractional dimensions, in fractal mathematics, which turn out to have real practical applications in, for instance, the mapping of geographical coastlines and the theory of electrical power.

However, within the debate there is a clear warning to be careful whenever anybody talks of what God may be like. With that in mind let us look at some current accounts of what God does and what God may be like.

Creation of the Universe

People seem always to want to know how the things which they experience have come about, and in the absence of enough knowledge to answer the questions definitively they compose stories to serve instead.

The old creation stories, like the two quite different accounts in the book of Genesis (chapters 1 and 2), are good stories, among the best that could have been told in their time, with the knowledge and the understanding which people had then. Nevertheless I believe that for us the modern stories of the Big Bang, the physical evolution of the universe, and the biological evolution of life, give more credible accounts of events which probably led to the world which you and I know about.

> *Stephen Jay Gould, in* Bully for Brontosaurus, *has an essay entitled 'The Creation Myths of Cooperstown'. One of the Myths concerns baseball, a sport on which he is an expert. He describes the annual celebrations in Cooperstown, New York, of the creation of the game by*

Abner Doubleday in 1839. Then he outlines what he says is a better understanding of the evolution of baseball from English bat-and-ball games of centuries before. The majority of Americans he believes to be happily deluded creationists in this important respect. He goes on to ask (but not to answer) the deeper questions about why we so desperately want to have creation Myths even when they are plainly false.

The two biblical stories of the creation of the world were fashioned almost completely in the imagination of those who first told them, and for years they were repeated and believed as 'factual' because nobody had any other information to contradict them. The story is told differently these days, only because now we have better information. Yet, I believe, there are *inner meanings* of these and many of the other old stories, which remain as true now as they ever were. This means that the old stories can still be told, as indeed they are in churches, for those inner meanings, even when almost none of the surface details can any longer be believed to be true.

But there are, it seems, some people who remain convinced that the surface details of the old stories *must* be true, and therefore the modern stories must be false. Here again is the problem of our unwillingness, our near inability, to change religious convictions to which we have committed ourselves. I suspect also that in those people the fear of change to established beliefs goes much deeper than merely the pain of rejecting a previous commitment. There is also, I believe, a profound fear of losing not an image but a 'real', secure, reliable God who could be trusted to act always in the ways that the ancients believed, firmly and positively in control of a world specifically created for humankind to work in and manage – and a fear therefore of replacing that God (or I should say, that image of God) with something far less secure.

Continuous Creation

The universe appears to have expanded continuously since the Big Bang, entirely, I believe, according to the Principles of Existence which were there from the beginning. The process, it now appears, has been one of continuous *self*-creation within those rules, without interference from any forces outside the system. The galaxies, the planet we live on, all living creatures, the human species itself, and our own individual lives, have evolved and developed 'naturally', in stages, out of possibilities which were inherent, but not specified in detail, from the very beginning. We can see now, when we look back over the sequence and deduce the patterns in it, the probable course which that development has taken, but we have far less success when we try to use the patterns to predict how things will develop in the future.

> *It is not yet clear to what extent the growth of complex systems and organisms may have come about through 'bottom-up creation', the association of individual components into new patterns, or to what extent the complex patterns develop first and work 'top-down' by drawing selected components into new combinations according to the pattern. From the predictions of Chaos Theory it appears that the latter route may well predominate. This raises some questions about the nature of the force behind creation, or the 'ways of God', if you prefer.*

God as Father

The metaphor of God as Father takes a central place in the beliefs of Christians, Jews, Muslims, and many others. With some reservations, I find it a good metaphor for the creative power of the universe. It does appear to be how that power was widely understood by pre-scientific people. It is the metaphor of a God who, like a good human father, provides all the necessities which his children cannot provide for themselves, lays down rules of behaviour with sanctions for breaking them, and is pleased when the children obey the rules, but gets angry when they do not.

It can be a good story still, especially for children whose experience of life is still largely the good experience of their own fathers or father-figures, though not for children for whom that experience is bad.

But I believe the story must be told differently among adults. For adults can do all of the things which once they needed father

to do. Often enough they can do them better. Adults can provide
their own needs for food, clothing, and shelter (or at least they
know how to), and can set their own rules of behaviour. I am also
sure that we ought to see that the human race itself is beginning
to grow up from an earlier childhood stage. We can now, literally,
do all kinds of things for ourselves which people in earlier ages
expected to be done by God. We can make any substance or any
article which the laws of physics and chemistry allow. If we want
to visit Venus we need only to find the money, make a vehicle and
go, with no need to ask permission from any father God. We know
we can make human laws, and expect and oblige people to obey
them, independently of what anyone may want to do about any
laws of God.

> *We are not sure that we ought to do all the things which are now pos-*
> *sible and we are aware that we do not always do enough of some of*
> *the things which we believe we should. But these are different questions.*

Now, what is the proper relationship of *grown-up* sons and
daughters, with the ability to manage all the practical necessities
of life for themselves, even to create and bring up their own suc-
cessors, with a Father who may still be there but is no longer *needed*
in the old way? A relationship of grateful, respectful independence? It never can be one of equality, for Father came first, we owe
so much to Father. But what Father is, the children inherit. Eventually, all children must take their own responsibility both for what
Father has given them and for what they will make of it. That
seems to me a proper attitude for well brought up adults.

I often hear it said in churches that we are 'children of God',
'made in the image of God', 'inheritors of the Kingdom of God'.
Less often do I hear that every child already possesses some at
least of the parent's characteristics and some of the parent's
powers, may be expected to come increasingly to behave in the
parent's ways, and will eventually come into whatever inheritance
the parent will leave.

But perhaps the growing up of human society as a whole has
by now reached only an adolescent stage. We are conscious of

enormous powers, we are fascinated but frightened by them, most unsure how to manage and control them, deeply embarrassed in not knowing how to conduct our changing selves among our companions and the rest of the world, and unhappy to admit either our ignorance or our fear. I believe that society will grow through this phase, though not until long after my time. Meanwhile, we continue to suffer all the embarrassments, the confusions, and the fears of our adolescence.

God as Mother

The story of God as Father has been told since at least the time of Abraham (around 2000 BCE, some say). But stories of God as Mother are older than that.

The time when Hebrew religion, with the other religions of the ancient world, began to take shape was also the time when the biological role of a father in the birth of children was only just becoming appreciated. Before, there could be no doubt that women were the bearers of the future, and therefore the ones who should control the present in the best interests of the future. So societies were matriarchal, as in some parts of the world until recently they still were. After, the men, who had at last discovered the essential part that fathers play in making the future, seized control of the present also and societies became patriarchal. Old creation stories, in which mother-gods and earth-gods create the future from within themselves and care for their creation in motherly ways, gave way to new stories of father-gods who create and control their creation, in intrusive, dominating, masculine ways. Many of the biblical stories of the struggles of Israelites with Caananites are stories also of the battles of the invading masculine God with the ancient established feminine ones. (And history, remember, including biblical history, is told by the victors to the denigration of the vanquished.)

Ever since then societies have been organized and controlled by men, and the religious stories have been masculine, told by men and for men. Women, if they heard them at all, had to hear and repeat them in the forms dictated by men.

This patriarchal system persisted until the sexual revolution of our time, until the practical possibility for every woman to control reproduction, and therefore her part in the future, *herself.* For Philip Larkin, until 1963, all had been bargaining, wrangle, and shame. (See his poem 'Annus Mirabilis' in *High Windows.*) Now we all know, in theory and in practice, though we may not all admit it, that the future is not under the control of men only or of women only, but of women and men together. Both are essential, neither is absolute. Creation, the making of the future, is a co-operative affair.

My women friends tell the God-as-Mother story better that I can, for it is their story, but I believe that what they tell is true. I believe in God as Father and I believe in God as Mother. But I do not believe that either story is the whole truth.

God as Trinity

The Athanasian Creed begins (in the Book of Common Prayer): "Whosoever will be saved: before all things it is necessary that he hold the Catholick Faith. And the Catholick Faith is this: That we worship one God in Trinity, and Trinity in Unity."

This is one of the two fundamental statements of the Christian faith. (The other is the statement that Jesus Christ is the Son of God, which we must consider presently.)

I believe that the statement refers to things even more widespread than Christian faith, to a fundamental three-ness of things which is to be found everywhere.

Hegel's dialectic proclaims it: every *thesis* leads to and permits an opposite *antithesis*. Both may simultaneously be true, yet they stand together and can be reconciled, under some tension, in a new and greater *synthesis* which transcends and combines them both.

The Principles of Existence which I see running through and underlying, in general and detail, all of the science, the technology, the training, the food technology which I know, are dialectic in form:

  − the thesis (everything has its identity, yet everything changes) describes the creation and existence of everything that is;

- the antithesis (every change has a cost) declares the paradoxical necessity that every creative step involves also destruction and loss;
- the synthesis (order and freedom come together) reconciles these opposites together, into new, richer, and more complex forms.

Similar triplets, of creation, conflict, and resolution, are to be seen in all kinds of relationships:

- in Newton's mechanical science, Action-Reaction-Movement form just such a triplet;
- so do the Attraction-Repulsion-Orbit of the physical chemist or the astronomer;
- in human affairs Father-Mother-Child is such a triplet, so is Man-Woman-Marriage or Woman-Man-Relationship;
- within us are our Id-Superego-Ego and the Body-Mind-Spirit which the ancients knew.

So, strikingly, is the Christian declaration of Trinity, of how reality is:

- Father/Creator of all that is;
- Son/Redeemer, the human embodiment of all the conflicts of experience;
- Spirit/Sustainer, the understanding and the strength in which everything is done and in which all paradoxes and difficulties are transcended.

The Christian doctrine of the Trinity developed in the early centuries CE, not apparently from direct recognition of the three-ness which I describe (though that is where they eventually arrived), but as Greek thinkers struggled to understand the philosophical implications of the other statement they wished to make, that "Jesus Christ is the Son of God." Some of the implications of their Father-Son-Spirit terminology, and much uncertainty in the meaning of some of the other words they used, caused fierce and unruly debates, but led ultimately to the official statements which we now call the Creeds.

Some of the phrases in those creeds present great difficulty today to me and to many of my Christian friends. For myself, I think I can see some way through the surface meaning of the words used to the inner realities which I believe those fourth- and fifth-century Greek-speakers were trying to express. But I don't believe that exercise should be necessary for every other modern day questioner.

In recent years new ways have been found to express these and other fundamental truths in words more acceptable to the modern mind. Examples are the description of the elements of the Trinity as Source of all being, Eternal Word, and Holy Spirit; or as God-beyond-us, God-beside-us and God-within-us.

I do believe that the need is urgent for the Church as a whole, in her worship and proclamations but also in her thinking, to relax the largely automatic use of the ancient formulae and replace them with more meaningful modern ones.

7

God and Humanity

Jesus of Nazareth

The outstanding contribution of the Christian faith to the understanding of life is the belief that, if there is a God at all, and whatever God may be like, or may do or not do, that God is active in all of human life.

Jesus of Nazareth was, I believe, a man who believed that truth about God, who knew what he believed and who lived his whole life *as if* it was true. At every step, I believe, he *chose* to be and to act in exactly the ways that he understood God to be and to act. At every point in his adult life he behaved *as if* he, a human, had nevertheless the same concerns as God and, within the limitations of being human, the same powers as God. This is exactly the attitude I have described as proper for a grown-up son to a loved and respected father.

Almost all of what I know about Jesus comes from the Bible, as the Bible is understood by modern scholars. I don't want here to go into how modern interpretations modify the 'plain meaning of the written text (what might be meant by 'walking on water', for instance) but for those who may not be familiar with those things here is a brief note.

The Gospel stories about Jesus, the scholars tell us, appear to have been written some forty or more years after Jesus's death. Some of the material in them may have been eye-witness accounts, but presented, inevitably, only as what was remembered and worked over by the time of writing. Much consists of stories which must have been spread for some time by word of mouth ('gossiping the gospel') and written down only later on. Some appears to have been constructed, sensitively and intelligently, to demonstrate points which individual authors wished to make, and some is plainly borrowed or invented to say how some things 'must have been' when nobody actually knew. One example is the different genealogies of Jesus and the nativity stories in Luke's and Matthew's Gospels. So it is doubtful whether more than a very few of the sayings attributed to Jesus, and only some of the happenings, can be believed certainly to have been said or to have happened exactly like that. What we have rather are accounts of events, as interpreted by people greatly affected by those events and their aftermath, and who then could not help telling the stories in the light of what had happened afterwards. Inevitably also, the assumptions behind the stories, about the nature of the world, the causes of sickness, the existence of angels and devils, and so on, were those which were commonly held at that time, most of them very different from the assumptions and beliefs of our time.

Now the God that Jesus knew, however he may have described the truth of it, to himself or to others, in metaphors and stories which were believable at *that* time, is the same God that I believe, however I may try to describe the truth of it, in stories which I want to be believable today.

For there is only one God: that must be the same for me as for Jesus. It must also be the same God as a scientist may describe:

the Source that (probably, we think) started everything off, but that now allows everything to develop 'by itself', interdependently with everything else and according to certain basic Principles.

All of the natural world, so far as I can see, already exists, develops, changes, and grows *like that*. Only the human species has much power of choice in the matter. Only humans have the capacity, and use it, to choose to act as they see fit, not necessarily in ways which may be the ways of God, the Way which Jesus chose to follow.

But what is it that is so special about Jesus? And what exactly is that Way?

Christ

Christ is risen! the Christians say. That, I believe, is what is so special. The God-ness which people saw in Jesus of Nazareth is alive now, after that man's death, everywhere. (It was alive and visible *before* Jesus' time too, though that is less often said.)

The stories tell how Jesus of Nazareth, whom some it seems, even in his lifetime, called the Christ (the Anointed One, the Messiah) was crucified, dead and buried. Shortly afterwards something extraordinary, astounding, and barely believable happened, which the people to whom it happened could describe only by saying that the man they knew to have been killed was now alive – but in a different way from before – and that they had met him. People have argued ever since about what exactly it was that caused them to say such things, but that *something* did, I do not doubt. Another short while after, a man called Saul of Tarsus, later called Paul, fell to the ground in what he swore later was an encounter with the same risen Christ. As he related it (three times the story is repeated in the New Testament) it was a meeting on a spiritual plane, but with dramatic physical and practical effects. He was temporarily blinded and it changed the whole direction of his life.

I cannot say myself that I have had such an experience of meeting Christ as directly as those people say they did, and as some of my acquaintances say that they have, 'in a flash' or however. It does seem rather as if the same Christ might have crept upon me quietly while I wasn't looking. I do know now that I believe what the others came to believe and I am happy to say it in the same words: Christ is risen!

That is first of all a statement about a *spiritual* reality, and I am sure that it is only through an experience of my spirit that I am able to make it. But it has outcomes, as there were for Paul, in the worlds of my physical and mental activity.

It is a statement also about a reality which is universal, going far beyond my experiences, or those of Paul or of any other person. Christ and God are co-eternal, con-substantial, sings one of the hymns. The God-ness, not only of humankind but of the whole of creation, has been there always, from their beginnings. Jesus of Nazareth, the man, knew that, revealed it, embodied it even; but it was so before he was born and it continues after his death, everywhere and in everything. Or so I see and believe.

New Birth

Now that I am aware of that spiritual truth, that Christ is alive, that God-ness exists in all things and all people, how shall I *act* on it? How *can* I choose to act as I believe Jesus did and as Christ inspires, in ways which conform with God's way, the way which is and has always been the natural way of the rest of the universe?

For there is a big problem. I may say that God's way is the way of the universe and ought to be my way too, but from my own point of view (which, remember, is the only point where I can start from) it definitely isn't. My reactions to anything are the reactions of *my* self. The choices which I have to make are about what I shall do with *my* life. But if I am to be able to do anything I must first guard, respect and maintain *that* life – *mine*. Yet it is plain that the interests of the rest of the universe are different from mine, and that from every other point of view save my own, my interests are relatively unimportant. Nobody and nothing else gives the priority to my concerns which I do. Everybody and everything else, inevitably, gives greater priority to their own concerns, their own existence, than to mine. How shall I choose to live in the interests of the rest of creation when most of those interests are so plainly different from mine?

This I take to be the essential problem of human morality: How can I live in dynamic, creative relationships with all the others whose interests are different from mine, even opposed to mine?

When a certain Nicodemus asked that question, in effect, so the story goes, Jesus replied, "Don't you know? You must be born again."

At my physical birth, under a compulsion to which I might have contributed but which I could not control, I was forced out from the safe, comfortable place where I had been provided with everything I needed to live and grow so far. I emerged into a completely different world where I had to begin to live for myself. From then on, my babyhood, childhood, and youth were occupied in discovering, developing, and extending the powers of *my* body and *my* mind, in establishing, as far as I was able, *my own* identity. Through all that time others continued to give me, mostly without my doing much about it, all of the nourishment and support and opportunities that I needed, and all for my development.

But sooner or later the growing adult is invited to make the choice: whether, or how far, to continue in the dependent childhood state, trusting that the necessaries of life will continue to be provided, as of right, by someone or from somewhere else, or whether to accept independence and begin to take responsibility for it all oneself. In the image described in the previous chapter, this means growing out of childhood dependence on Father and accepting the adult responsibility of managing an inheritance from Father. Or in the image just used, it means leaving behind the safety and comfort in which life has grown so far, and forcing oneself out, with pain and difficulty, into a new, different, and as yet unknown life.

> *Encouragement and help may be given but essentially the new birth has to be done for oneself, and it can be. The English verb 'to be born' is passive, as if birth is something which must happen to the child. But surely the child, already alive in the womb, also plays a part in*

choosing the time and summoning the forces to get itself born. The French verb is active, something which the infant does – naître, to birth.

In the new life of independence the priority is no longer, as it quite properly was before, the development of *my* body, done for me in the womb, nor the discovery and strengthening of *my* powers of body and mind in childhood and youth, but my *use* of those powers, however weak or strong I may think them, to *participate* in the spirit and in the continuing creation of the whole universe.

But I have to make the switch. If I don't, I cannot live in God's way. And I have to *choose* to make it. I think that is the most important choice one ever has to make.

A note about Born Again Christians. I think that people who describe themselves so do not usually mean quite the same as I say here. It seems to me that they mostly want to say that they have encountered the truth of Jesus and are greatly moved by it. "I welcomed the Lord Jesus Christ into my life," is one way it may be put. This may be an admirable state to be in, but it is one which, I suspect, can only be preliminary to the deliberate and rather painful process which I call New Birth.

Christ and God

The man Jesus of Nazareth was, I believe, filled to overflowing with God-ness. In his lifetime there must been many who recognized that and said, as we might say, "This is a man of God," or "This is a son of God." At that time this was not an unusual name to give a holy man. Those who saw him also as the Messiah, the expected deliverer of the Jewish people, might even have said, "This is *the* Man of God."

It does seem from the biblical record that Jesus himself was reluctant to agree to any such titles, accepting only 'son of man', roughly equivalent to 'an ordinary person'. One passage reads, " 'But you,' he asked, 'who do you say that I am?' Peter spoke up and said to him, 'You are the Christ'." (Mark 8:29) He gave them strict orders not to tell anyone about him. Or, "You had better not say that to anyone else."

After Jesus's death there were certainly people who saw and said those things increasingly. Then as the years passed, with the human Jesus no longer around to be seen and questioned, but instead with inexplicable, vivid, and compelling experiences of his continuing presence, and the growing belief that in some way the *spirit* of that man, alive again after his terrible death, is the way the whole world can and ought to be (the way the world will be 'saved'), the descriptions and titles changed further. The move was from simile, "This man is like what God must be like," to metaphor, "This man is God."

It happened quickly. Only about twenty-five years after Jesus's death, Paul writes, quoting from a contemporary hymn: "His state was divine but he did not cling to his equality with God..." (Philippians 2:6). So also, John in the meditations he incorporated into his Gospel, another two or three decades later, has Jesus repeatedly saying, "I am...[something profoundly Godly]..."

So all the long wrangles of Christian doctrine began: about the nature of Christ, the substance of God, the means of salvation, and the punishments for those who fail to believe 'correctly'.

But now? For me?

I believe that all metaphors and stories of God are inventions of the human imagination, inevitably anthropomorphic. I cannot believe that God might be limited by any properties which I am able to comprehend. I believe that any permanent parent-infant relationship is inadequate for adult people and quite unworthy of God. So what do I make of Christ?

I do believe that here, so far as can be seen from any human perspective, is a glimpse of how God *is*. In Christ I see the human face of God.

Christ as the *spirit* of that man who *as a man* knew and understood how God *is* and who himself behaved accordingly at all times – that Christ, living still, I believe and trust. I want to follow in his Way, to live *like that*. It is how the earliest followers of Jesus were described, "those who follow in *the Way*". It was only at Antioch, ten years or so after Jesus died, "that the disciples were first called 'Christians' ." (Acts 11:26)

What is that Way, put simply? I believe it can be expressed in two heavily loaded words: Acceptance and Sacrifice.

Acceptance

If everything has its identity (Principle 1), if everything has, and is entitled to, its own value, its own degree of freedom, its own interests and priorities, why do we find that in practice so difficult to accept? Why do we allow some things or people lower status than others, why do we call some things 'faults', some behaviour 'sinful'?

> *What is the San Andreas Fault? Why do we call it a fault? Whose fault is it, what makes it a fault?*

Faults with things

Start with the natural world. Faults are natural things which just happen to be different from the other natural things around them which get called 'normal'. Statisticians call them deviations from the norm, and go on to calculate the Standard Deviation of any collection of things, events, facts, and measurements – the extent to which any individual can be found to deviate from the average of the whole collection. The universe contains many and vast collections of things, all with normal distributions (or some variant of the normal distribution) and standard deviations. Every distribution has its extremes, its outliers, its deviants. The deviants, inevitably, because they *are* different, behave differently from the rest, react differently to the circumstances around them.

Here lie the causes of what we call 'natural disasters'. Earthquakes in California for instance are only occasional extreme instances of the 'normal' variations in the relationship between the earth's crust and its interior, of forces which are not yet understood very well. Science long ago *accepted* that these things are natural occurrences, and set about finding causes and trying to understand, allow for, and where possible to anticipate and control them.

Blame, Guilt and Forgiveness

Stay with the natural world with its earthquakes, volcanoes, floods, collisions with meteors, preying animals, and insect-eating flowers. In no case is the natural world to be *blamed* for what goes on, even on the most violent occasions. There is nothing for any part of the natural world to feel *guilty* about. There is nothing to *forgive*.

Or is there? If I should say that *Forgiveness is the declaration that what has happened, with all its consequences however violent and painful, is accepted as fact, with all its natural causes and effects*, then there might be a sense in which the natural world, automatically and implicitly accepting the facts, causes, and effects of its own behaviour as within the normal pattern of things, thereby equally automatically 'forgives' itself for the consequences.

But really, blame, guilt, and forgiveness are human concepts which properly apply only when humans and human feelings are involved.

Faults with people

As with dirt, which my mother used to say is only matter in the wrong place (before she made me wash mine off), natural faults of any kind are usually more or less inconvenient and sometimes harmful to people affected by them. It is the inconvenience and the harm, to themselves or others, to which people react and which often lead them to complain that faults or dirt or accidents 'ought' not to happen. They *feel* that something is wrong and feel angry about it; and the *feelings* of wrong and of anger may be stronger than the pain of whatever actual hurt has been caused. This is so especially when people perceive that the faults are caused or permitted by others, and more especially when they believe that the faults should have been avoidable, that they ought not to have been done or permitted at all. The strongest feelings of all may even come not directly from the actual hurt but indirectly, from hurt to people's *ideas* of what *ought* to be normal.

Those who cause or permit faults to happen, deliberately or accidentally or unknowingly, may or may not feel shame and guilt about it. But the affected ones, to relieve their own feelings, may want to find someone to blame, to hold responsible, to consider guilty. So any guilt which is felt by the perpetrators of harm may be increased as the hurt ones project their own bad feelings onto them. The total guilt, as long as it remains, is the greatest inhibitor of the freedom of any of the parties to act reasonably, let alone generously, in the future.

Religious people will commonly describe the doing or the permitting as sins, others may call them crimes. Yet the people whose behaviour is thus marked as sinful or criminal have almost always chosen, consciously or unconsciously, to do what they did for reasons which appeared good to them at the time. They followed what they understood to be in their own best interest in the circumstances as they saw them. Bruno Bettelheim, out of his personal and professional experience, wrote that, "…whatever [a person's] behaviour, it would seem the most natural thing for me were I in the other's situation. I believe it was this conviction that permitted me, years later, to understand the behaviour of the SS guards in the concentration camps, and this understanding helped me greatly to survive being there." (From his essay 'How I Learned about Psychoanalysis', in *Recollections and Reflections*.)

Sinners or criminals might have acted without regard for others and without proper adult responsibility, but in the vast majority of cases both the things which they did and their motives for doing them, however unwelcome to 'normal' people, will have had 'natural' causes, and may justly be seen as unusual but 'natural' deviations from what the others consider 'normal'.

As with things in the natural world, some deviants may indeed be destroyed because of their abnormality, others may continue to live, coping with it; some rare ones may become the beginnings of entirely new and unexpected things (which of course is how natural selection works); but few of them, however inconvenient or hurtful to others, are themselves intrinsically *wrong*.

The guilt of any of these faults or deviations might be removed by the passage of time, if all the parties gradually forget what the trouble was, but that is not very common. For a vivid example, look only at more than three centuries of unforgotten hurts and hatreds in Ireland, only now beginning to be addressed. Most usually, people can be freed from their guilt and their feelings of guilt only by the exercise of forgiveness.

Here is how forgiveness works:
— all involved, hurters, hurt ones, and bystanders, with proper respect for one another's circumstances, must *accept* the facts of the hurt, of whatever and various kinds, that has been done and suffered;
— each must *accept* proper responsibility for their own part in causing the hurt and mark the acceptance with recompense if possible, but always with some gesture of contrition;
— then those who caused hurt may ask forgiveness from those who suffered it;
— the hurt ones must offer their forgiveness (they might even offer it unasked);
— the perpetrators must accept it;
— the completion of the process is normally to be marked with another gesture, this time of reconciliation.

Then all can get on again with living together – not 'as if nothing has happened', for serious things have, but in the knowledge that with the past accepted and forgiven, and the present repaired as well as we are able, we can now all go forward from where we are, freed from all the old anger and guilt.

Of course, the acceptance has to be complete, on both sides. Refusal to accept the necessity of any stage in the process, however difficult and painful, blocks off the rest and leaves everyone still with the anger, the guilt, and the hostility.

This is how Jesus acted. He would never withhold forgiveness, nor the healing which follows it, from anyone who would recognize the fault and its harmfulness, be willing to make reparation if that were possible, and to change behaviour in future – that is, to 'repent'. Jesus, it appears, looked upon all the human failings, all the faults and the dirt about which people feel guilty and are made to feel guilty, as understandable, 'natural' deviations from the normal, therefore forgivable. He never seems to have asked about causes, only accepted each situation, checked if necessary that the person did recognize that the fault and the dirt were there, that there was something to be sorry about, to wash, to adjust if possible, and to cope with if not. To all such people his response was the same: "Your sins are forgiven." You are accepted. To those paralyzed, crippled, blinded, deafened by the guilt they suffered because of their deviations from the norms around them, he would add, "You are well, you are healed already, go, pick up your bed, walk, see, hear, get on with your life…"

Working examples

I believe that understanding and applying this twin process of acceptance and forgiveness is absolutely critical to the business of living together with other people in a world where faults and deviations and conflicts of interest are quite inevitable. Let me add a couple of direct examples out of my food technology experience.

The greater part of my work has been in food quality control and quality assurance, where I see the operation of precisely these processes. In that profession we *expect* that whatever anybody or any machine does and however carefully, especially when it is done on a large scale, there will inevitably be some deviations, errors, and defects. There can be variations in sizes, shapes, colours, weights; omissions or variations in formulations; errors in descriptions, labels, orders, deliveries, and accounts; misjudgements of policy and regulation. We learn to recognize all these and more, to measure them when they occur, not to deny them, overlook them, or hide them, but to accept them as fact when we find them or someone else points them out. If harm has been done, we do what we can to correct or compensate. We seek, but do not always find, ways to prevent or to minimize the size or the frequency of the faults in future. And when all that is done, recorded, and reported, we do know that the past faults, from whatever causes, can be forgiven, that there is no need to continue to carry guilt for them, that we are all now free to get on with the next job, to make the next dozen or thousand or million of similar things, as well as we can.

Outside the industry and the profession, however, there are those who withhold forgiveness from those they hold responsible for some of the defects and variations in our processes. They fear, reasonably or unreasonably, for the consequences to themselves or others of factory farming, salmonella, BSE, E numbers, obesity, genetically modified foods – to take only a few from the list. I will not attempt here to argue the case for an industry which I believe to act responsibly in these matters. That is done very fully elsewhere by colleagues I respect. I see something else underlying it all: the projection of deep fears, some real, some imagined (and perhaps not all related to food), on to a convenient and relatively 'soft' target – the food industry and its public administration. But what seems so often to be lacking is *acceptance* by those harmed, or concerned about harm to others, that the problems are indeed known (imperfectly of course) to those who take responsibility, seriously, for their resolution, and that they are cared about and are attended to as well as current knowledge permits, errors and misjudgements notwithstanding (and yes, commercial or political self-interest sometimes too). The professionals also, perhaps from their better knowledge of many of the facts, may fail to accept the strength of the fears of the complainants. But without such acceptance, on both sides, it cannot be possible for either party to ask forgiveness or offer it to the other. Without forgiveness none of us can get on with the greater purposes of life, enjoying all that is good in our food even as we try to deal sensibly with its more troublesome imperfections.

I take some issue here with colleagues who say that these difficulties could be resolved through greater education of the public. I'm not so sure. The guilt and the fears are not only in the mind, where education might have some benefit, but deeper, in the psyche, the spirit, where they stay relatively unaffected by information or logical argument. That raises a different question.

Who is there who can minister at all the levels – practical, intellectual and psychological/spiritual – to enable the necessary understanding, acceptance and forgiveness?

Sacrifice

It is a fundamental claim of Christianity that *through* the sacrifice of Christ, *through* the Cross of Christ, we are saved, we come to new life. Christians say that in Jesus and in the way of his life, most particularly in the way he chose to complete his life, we see the working out of exactly the principles of the God that he believed in, and which we are invited to follow. While acceptance and the forgiveness which follows it are critical to the life of humans together, as Jesus showed, sacrifice and the suffering which accompanies it are necessary too, as Jesus also showed.

There is something more: sacrifice is one of the fundamental Principles of Existence. Every change has its cost, everything new and good is made from something else which itself also was good, everything eventually dies (is sacrificed), yet is carried forward to make new life, and can be discovered afterwards in that new state (resurrected) under a completely new form, usually unexpected and at first unrecognized – as in the story of the resurrection of Jesus.

Many Christians, and others, have difficulty with the notion that Christ's suffering and sacrifice are supposed to have *done* something *for* us. But the notion and the difficulties, I believe, arise from inadequate *images* of what God may be like – such as that terrible image of a father with an 'only' son, requiring 'recompense' for all the sins which people other than the son have committed.

Start rather with Jesus as an extraordinary man, a 'son of man' as he modestly used to say, filled with God-ness and the understanding of God's ways. Then perhaps what Christ *does* for us, through that story of Jesus, is to open our eyes and our understanding to see the proper place of sacrifice, and its cost, in all the life of the universe, and to understand that this is, was, and always will be the way of things, the way of God. Then we may find, or be given, the strength to follow in the same way ourselves.

This is a truth about Reality, about the whole of existence:

All life comes about only through the sacrifice of other life; everything good in creation comes about through the sacrifice of something else which was itself good.

Here is how it works, in that most elementary chemical equation:

$$2\ H_2\quad +\quad O_2\quad \longrightarrow\quad 2\ H_2O$$

pure   *pure*   *BANG*   *pure water*
hydrogen *oxygen*   no more hydrogen
               no more oxygen

The pure water is a quite new thing, made of the old hydrogen and oxygen, but utterly different from either.

Recall some of the earlier examples and add others, first from the natural world:

 - life on this planet depends absolutely on the supply of energy from the sun, produced by the consumption, the sacrifice, of the substance of the sun itself;
 - plants take nitrogen from the air and minerals from the soil in order to live and grow, the air and the soil sacrificing some of their substance to enable it;
 - animals, including humans, can live only by consuming, by sacrificing, other living things – plants or animals;
 - the muscles of every animal move and the brain functions by the burning, the sacrifice, of carbohydrates and of fat that used to be part of its own body;
 - if any creature has to starve she first sacrifices the substance of her own body until almost none is left;
 - a hen deprived of calcium does the same, sacrificing calcium from her bones to ensure healthy shells on her eggs, until she dies herself from bone weakness and other side effects of calcium deficiency;

and then from human life:

 - the food which we eat was all of it produced by people who sacrificed their time and energy to do so (and the sacrifice is not diminished if afterwards they were paid – even adequately paid);

- every choice we make – to buy this, go there, do that – involves the sacrifice of one or more alternatives;
- at every great passage of life – going to school, first job, new job, marriage, retirement, bereavement – there are real sacrifices to be made, usually painful, and not only by the one making the passage, of the state we enjoyed before; if we fail to 'let go' of that state then the new state is sure to be less than satisfactory;
- almost every new idea requires the giving up of an old one, however useful the old one may have been and however dearly held.

If there is any purpose to existence it is *not that everything has some right to continue always in the same state but that everything is ultimately to give itself – to be willingly sacrificed – to participate in the continuing creation of whatever greater and richer existence is still to come.*

For you and me it is the same. The purpose of our existence is not that we shall go on for ever as we are, but that we shall contribute what we are now to the greater existence which is already around us and reaching forward into a greater, unknown future. But we have to choose to follow that Way. Failure to do so is indeed, I believe, the way of death. It is not that our own physical death will come any sooner or more unpleasantly, but that our share in all the possibilities of new and richer life in the future will be stillborn.

Human Choice

The human species appears to have evolved in the same ways as all other creatures, in the interplay of apparently randomly happenings in climate and geography, according to the same rules of genetics and natural selection, and in relationship with the development of all the other creatures around. Over a wide range of our personal and private activities we follow automatically the same laws of nature, the same Principles of Existence as apply to every other animal, vegetable, and mineral.

There are of course a few subsidiary rules or principles pecu-
liar to our own species, in our physiology and some of our psycho-
logy, for instance, including one of over-riding importance. With
humans something extra has evolved: the capacity for reflective,
subjective thought, and a consequent greatly enhanced freedom
of choice in our actions, compared with any other creature.
Unlike all other creatures, over a wide range of our activities,
including almost all of our relationships with one another and the
rest of the universe, in economics and sociology and politics and
ethics and morality, humans are able to make their rules and to
choose whether and how far to follow them.

To the extent that we choose to make our rules in the same
pattern as the Principles of Existence, our human behaviour can
be in harmony with that of the rest of existence. Christians say
that the pattern is most clearly displayed in the life and death of
Jesus and the continuing life of Christ. I will add that the same
pattern is to be seen everywhere, if you look.

All of us, always, have the choice to make, to choose to undergo what I described earlier as New Birth, to switch from our
immediate self-centred inclinations, to recognize that other way as
natural and right, and to follow it as best we can. When everyone
does that, I believe we shall have reached the state which Jesus
called the Kingdom of Heaven. Meanwhile, most of the time we
don't choose to go that way: we prefer to follow some other set of
principles, some other god.

Part 3:
Implications

❖ ❖ ❖ ❖ ❖ ❖ ❖ ❖ ❖ ❖ ❖ ❖ ❖ ❖ ❖

8

Today's Gods

My God

I have tried to describe the best image which I can make today of the God in which I do believe, my best model of how Reality Is, with features consistent so far as I can see with everything else which I know, believe, and feel to be true in all of my scientific, technological, and other experience. It is the model I have tried to describe in the previous chapters. I cannot pretend it to be anything like a complete or perfect representation of the True God that I do believe to exist but it is the best I can do. I presume to call it, here at any rate, 'My God'.

This God is an energy or a force which has been behind the universe from the beginning, however that was, that 'set everything going', and then 'left it all' to develop 'by itself' according to some basic and universal rules which may be described as Principles of Existence.

I believe in the way in which that force operates in the universe of which I am a part, most notably in:
- the fact of the existence and activity, the incompleteness and inter-relatedness of all that is, at every instant, with the variability which is normal among the individuals in every group;
- the changeability of everything, always at the cost of other changes.

I believe that that force, and the Principles of Existence through which it operates, extends in all dimensions and beyond everything I may know or could know. Especially do they apply in all human activity, and I believe that the freedom which we have as humans is most properly exercised when we adopt the same

Principles for ourselves, by:

- – accepting that every thing and person is somewhere in the creative process of coming about, existing in company and then passing on; that each has only a small, incomplete and defective knowledge of any of the others, and no certain knowledge of what is going to happen in the future;
- – accepting the existence, the freedom, and the right to exist of every thing and person that is; the need to accommodate ourselves with the others, however inconvenient or noisome we find one another; and the ultimate necessity to give our own existence to the furtherance of the rest;
- – accepting that whatever freedom we may wish to enjoy must be limited at some points by the freedom required by others; that whatever order we may wish to promote must be limited at some points by the exercise of relative freedom by others.

This is also the Christian faith. We believe in One God, one ultimate reality:

- – Creator, source of all that is;
- – Redeemer, embodiment of the Way in which all paradoxes and conflicts are to be resolved, in acceptance and mutual respect, and in willing sacrifice;
- – Spirit, sustainer, uniting all in common understanding and purpose, in a delicate balance of order and freedom.

But not everyone sees things like this. Many believe in and follow other 'gods'.

No God

There was no creation, say the atheists, and so there is no need to suppose a Creator. There is no First Cause beyond our ability to think. Everything 'just happens' and it always has. Even the Big Bang need not have been the first thing. It might only be the follower of the Big Crunch at the end of a previous existence, and Big Crunch and Big Bang will go on repeating from the end of this existence and into infinity. Even so, if creation should turn out to be infinitely continuous, that would still leave the question why it exists at all – to which, for me, 'God' is a reasonable answer.

There are also those who say that there is no Beyond in which a god might be encountered by any of the real components of the universe. There is no Spirit, nothing beyond our science and our minds, they say; everything is or will be explainable by the science we already know or can expect to know in future.

Some say that this is where the conflict between science and religion lies. But I do not see this as a real conflict, only an argument about definitions. Is there Spirit or is there not? If there is, science and religion are two possible ways of regarding reality. If not, then religion in any of its present forms is meaningless. And I have set out why I think it reasonable to believe that there is Spirit.

Besides, I suspect that relatively few people take the extreme atheist view. Numerous opinion surveys, and my own observation, conclude that among the many people who profess no formal religious commitment there is a high proportion who do admit to some implicit religious beliefs and practices – belief for instance in some kind of Divine Power, to whom indeed they may pray at least occasionally. (See Alister Hardy and his classic work *The Spiritual Nature of Man*, on the religious experiences of a wide variety of people, whether they claim to profess any religion or none.)

I do not think therefore that belief in No God poses any great threat to a human understanding of ourselves and our condition, or to our private or public ways of life. Or, at any rate, it is not as great a threat as those of some other gods.

False God – the God of Private Benefit

This is the False God, well-nigh universal, which informs almost all of the economics, politics, and social organization of our present world, across all cultures and even many religious systems.

It is the god of adult people, who have and use all of the powers available to them, but selfishly. Their outlook on the rest of reality has stuck in the self-centred stage of infancy. They have not made the 'New Birth' switch from self-centredness to participation in the rest of creation, and they appear to have no intention of doing so.

Under that False God people can believe that everything outside themselves is provided for their particular benefit, to satisfy all that they consider they need. So they think it entirely right to take whatever comes as entitlement, and appropriate and use it entirely for their own purposes. They need not take any special care for the needs of others, for the others should employ the same right to look after themselves. Instead they need take care only that nobody takes from them any of the things which have come to them through the workings of that god and his ways.

The economics of Adam Smith, of Reagan and Thatcher, and of most of the world's very wealthy are of exactly this sort. So are the politics of Machiavelli and almost all kings, presidents, and governments. Some speak occasionally of wealth 'trickling down' or power being shared, but the talk does not usually carry any implication that what the speakers already hold might be significantly diminished. The world at the beginning of the twenty-first century possesses astonishing wealth, and the managers of our society wield enormous powers. But who besides the holders of these things is allowed to share them?

Sometimes I hear Jesus's parable of the talents quoted in justification. (Matthew 25:14–30 and Luke 19:12–26 both tell it, with small differences in detail.) Three servants were given money to look after by their master who was going on a journey. One used his to make a large profit, one made a smaller profit, and one made none at all. On the master's return the first was highly commended and highly rewarded, the second was commended and rewarded, the third was berated and punished. The story is quoted to illustrate the workings of private enterprise and to justify the making of profit by those with the ability to do so.

However, modern tellers of the story usually omit to mention two significant features of Jesus's version. The money which the servants used was *provided for them* at the outset, in trust, and not by any kind of right; and even more importantly, *they kept none* of the profits but handed them over immediately to their master when he returned. The good servants in the parable did indeed show commendable enterprise, but they did not use it for their private benefit.

In our local, national and international politics, and in our community and ethnic relations, the same False God of Private Benefit rules. A proper love of one's country or neighbourhood or ethnic group is most usually understood only as self-centred seeking of the greatest benefit to the group, perhaps only to those in the group who are closest to ourselves, in wealth, power, or territory. Even in family and private life we are encouraged by most of those around us to believe that we have the right that our own wants should be satisfied first, and to insist upon that right, even if it means denying some of the rights of others.

Under this privatized, self-centred False God we can have no understanding of the possibility of new-life-through-willing-sacrifice, only of enterprise-for-profit-to-be-kept. So we cannot begin to see how to meet what is probably the greatest challenge to human life on this crowded planet, how to live peaceably with neighbours who have different opinions, desires, and requirements from ourselves; nor even the second and simpler challenge, how to manage the resources of the earth, what to consume, what to sacrifice, what to save, and what to grow. We fail to grow up ourselves, or to allow those around us to grow, into real freedom, into proper adult responsibility for one another, into richer life for all, and the hope of still richer life for those who will come after us.

Inadequate God – the God of Popular Religion

This is the image of god I hear widely proclaimed in Christian circles, and the one most widely believed by those outside the church to be the Christian God. It is not completely False and is certainly not No God, but neither does it have all the features of the True God in which I believe.

It is the god of people who, though they may have moved some way beyond infantile self-centredness, still do not choose to abandon the image of a god who represents the comfort and security of their childhood. They hold to the image of a father-god responsible for everything, always in control, provider of whatever is best for his children. He (masculine, of course) intervenes from time to time for particular purposes of his own, changing the course of nature by special favour on particular occasions, and he may even be induced sometimes to do so again if worthy people will ask him properly.

But belief in this Inadequate God, that life is or ought to be *like that*, has some important adverse consequences for the believer's outlook on life and behaviour.

First, if the creation is supposed to operate under this god's direct control of everything that happens, then that gives direct licence to those who follow that god for two opposite kinds of abuse. On the one hand, anyone with the necessary ability and opportunity may take direct control of a government, nation, school, company, family, or other group in society, and claim to control it in God's way and on God's behalf; they may even claim, as many an emperor, king, or bishop has, that what they do is 'God's will'. On the other hand, when the subjects of the ruler live under the same belief, that this is how things must be because their god has ordained it, their submission provides the very support which autocratic rulers need. Proper democratic rule, the acceptance by every adult member of the community of an appropriate share of the responsibility for its management, can hardly begin in such a climate.

> *This state of affairs does not have to persist. In my professional life I have seen and participated in the shift from quality* control *to quality* assurance. *That is, from production systems which were supposed to be controlled by an independent quality control department whose task was to seek out faults and, when they were found, to recommend corrective action and appropriate disposal of the defective items, to production systems set up to be self-controlling, with product and process specifications agreed in advance, including permitted tolerances for minor deviations, and procedures for the resolution of major ones. So the task of quality assurance is to do only a sufficient minimum of checks for everybody to be sure that everything is running to plan all the time.*

So I have seen and helped a piece of industry to shift in the direction which Archbishop William Temple once described as the direction towards Christ's Kingdom: from control of conduct by force, to control of heart and mind and will by love and truth.

Of course, not everything has gone that way. While many within the industry have moved from control to assurance, forces from outside have pressed powerfully in the other direction. Over recent years public and legal controls have become much more prescriptive, more confrontational.

Even where responsibility and power are more democratically shared, the tendency remains under this Inadequate God for people to prefer to have all authorities (in government and in the affairs of society), and all explanations (in the fields of knowledge and opinion and belief), provided for them ready-made and reliable. They prefer to be told 'officially' what is right, to be relieved of any need to decide for themselves. There are of course plenty of cases where we ought to give authority to others more competent to deal with particular things than we are. What usually happens however, even in those cases, is that we *give* authority to whoever claims the right, and the competence, to exercise it from above us, instead of *delegating* to them the exercise of our own responsibility. That way, we can feel free to complain about what the authority does or tells us, without having any need to accept responsibility ourselves for having allowed it.

Secondly, people are encouraged to ask for miraculous solutions to difficulties, to call on the imagined god to intervene and change the course of events that they think he must have planned. When no miracle occurs they say that the difficulty must have been God's will from the beginning, and so nothing more can be done about it. But miracles do not happen, or fail to happen, like that. To wish for them is to surrender our own capacity to change the things which can be changed and to accept and adjust to the things which cannot. So our ability to live positively is weakened.

I know of course that some people do pray for miracles to overcome local difficulties, and that when a difficulty is resolved they count that as proof that prayer to the miracle-making god is effective. "I prayed for a parking space and God found me one." But I don't believe it. Such things come about through the normal happenings of chance, not from the intervention of a childhood god that I no longer need.

So we try to surrender proper adult responsibility for the practical things of life, and to pass it instead to a mistaken idea of god or to some god-figure or authority-figure of our own appointment. There is also a deeper failure, to acknowledge our own status, along with that of every other creature, as *participants* together in all the affairs of creation, co-creators *with* God, as one of the Christian phrases has it. Deeper still is the failure to face the dark side of all these questions:

— fear of that Other which is the God whom we cannot fully know, only describe in images of our own making;

— fear of our own unknown and unknowable future, fear of the change from behaving like children to behaving as adults, and above all, fear of our own certain death;

— fear of our inevitable failure to get everything right, coupled with an inability or unwillingness to accept that almost all of our failures are forgivable, provided only that we acknowledge them;

— fear of accepting for ourselves the necessity of willing sacrifice in the present, only through which can the new and fuller life of the future come about.

Of course it is difficult for those religiously committed to the comfort and comparative certainty of this old but now inadequate god, to move towards the excitement, the freedom, and the responsibility represented by the true God. I grieve that so many in the churches seem so afraid to make the move, but until more of us do so we must all face the extra difficulty that this Inadequate God is the one which nearly all of the uncommitted think that we worship. When any of them says that he does not believe in God, it almost always seems to be this Inadequate God which he has heard Christians proclaim, that he does not believe. Similarly, what many see as the conflict between science and religion is usually only conflict with this inadequate and unscientific god, not with the true God that is far greater than either our science or our religion. So present and future Christians owe it not only to ourselves but to the rest of humanity, to make the leap of faith into adult belief in an infinitely more credible, more worthy, and more powerful God.

My Practice

I am now retired from most (not quite all) technological and consultancy work and from most (not quite all) local church activities. Still, I remain a food technologist and I remain a priest.

How do I stand then, holding the beliefs which I have described, in a Church which for the most part, so far as I can see, is inclined to proclaim some rather different beliefs? And most particularly, what do I say and do when I am asked, as I still am sometimes, to conduct or take part in a church service or other public church activity?

First, I can almost never know precisely what anybody else believes of God and what they may disbelieve. They may be ready to hear new suggestions; they may be encouraged by hearing some of their own ideas expressed by an ordained person; they may be hurt by any such suggestion. I do believe that many of us, perhaps all of us to some extent, and more than we can admit, are influenced by that self-centred False God of Private Benefit which is all around us. Many too appear unable or unwilling to move beyond the Inadequate God, still so widely proclaimed. Yet at the same time I suspect that there are many who in their minds and spirits do see beyond the falsity and the inadequacy to some of the grandeur of the Truth which I want to proclaim. They may not say it very much, they might not know how to say it, or perhaps they might if only they were given encouragement. But usually I cannot know any of this for certain. I can only try to listen carefully to what people say, and to the sub-text which they don't say.

Secondly, I do try myself in conversations, in preaching, and in some forms of public worship, to speak positively and only of the ways of God as I understand them. Those ways, as I have outlined them here, are, I believe, hopeful and encouraging accounts of all of the questions which the preacher or worshipper may need to speak of. With so much which is positive, so much Good News to tell, I am sure there is little need to speak of things which I don't believe, or to become entangled in arguments about how far the images which I or others use may be true or false.

Lastly, there is the question of formal liturgical services where the language, and even more the imagery behind the language, speak too directly of those False or Inadequate images of God which I believe to be harmful. The English *Book of Common Prayer*, still clung to by many, contains obvious examples. I make no secret among clergy colleagues of my reservations about it and, when they will listen, of my reasons. But the case is altered if I am faced with a request to take an occasional service for a congregation of people whom I do not know well. Then the proper course does seem to be to use the form of service with which they are familiar, not to risk causing damage which I should be unable to repair.

Here I ponder the meaning of some more words of Bruno Bettelheim, about "...the need and usefulness of acting on the basis of fictions that are known to be false..." He goes on to speak of his "philosophical conviction that we must live by fictions – not just to find meaning in life but to make it bearable." (From his essay 'Essential Books of One's Life', in *Recollections and Reflections*.) Is this what I meant when I wrote of the way in which a religious ceremony may speak directly to my spirit even while my mind wants to reject some of the surface meanings of the words and actions taking place?

Then I remember what I have said earlier, that every religious ceremony is intended above all to foster the *spiritual* encounter of all the participants with God, and that the encounter will never be bound only by the surface activities and meanings, or by the possible implications of some of the words. The Holy Spirit does guide us into Truth, through all our human clumsiness. The task of the priest is to promote and not to hinder that work of the Spirit, on behalf of everyone present, using the facilities available. I accept that task.

That also seems a good way to understand all that we all have to do in every other aspect of life: to live as if what is said, however haltingly, about the True God is indeed, all of it, true.

LIST OF BOOKS
REFERRED TO IN THE TEXT

Bettelheim, Bruno *The Uses of Enchantment: The Meaning and Importance of Fairy Tales*, Penguin Books, 1991.

Bettelheim, Bruno *Recollections and Reflections*, Penguin Books, 1992.

Campbell, Joseph *Myths to Live By: How we re-create ancient legends in our daily lives to release human potential*, Bantam Books, 1973.

Capra, Fritjof *The Tao of Physics*, Fontana, 1992.

Crowder, Colin (ed.) *God and Reality*, Mowbray, 1997.

Gould, Stephen Jay *Bully for Brontosaurus*, Hutchinson Radius, 1991.

Hammarskjöld, Dag *Markings* (translation by W. H. Auden & Leif Sjöberg), Faber, 1964.

Hardy, Alister *The Spiritual Nature of Man*, Clarendon Press, 1979.

Hofstadter, Douglas R. *Goedel, Escher, Bach: an Eternal Golden Braid*, Penguin Books, 1980.

Larkin, Philip *High Windows*, Faber and Faber, 1974.

The Mission Theological Advisory Group *The Search for Faith and the Witness of the Church*, Church House Publishing, 1996.

Robinson, John A. T. *Honest to God*, SCM Press, 1963.

Shaw, Graham *God in Our Hands*, SCM Press, 1987.